Tribal Government
Wind River Reservation

Tribal Government
Wind River Reservation

Written by Janet Flynn
A.W. Baldwin, contributor

Edited and updated by Shannon D. Smith
in partnership with WyoHistory.org

2026
WordsWorth Publishing
Cody, Wyoming

First edition published 1991, revised 1998
Second Edition 2026

ISBN: 979-8-9939600-0-5 (print)
ISBN: 979-8-9939600-1-2 (eBook)

Library of Congress Control Number: 2026932484

Cover: *Buffalo Spirits*, oil on canvas by Jon Cox

Published by WordsWorth Publishing, Cody, Wyoming
www.wordsworthpublishing.com

CONTENTS

FOREWORD TO THIS EDITION

The unique landscape of the Wind River Reservation exemplifies the resilience and history of the Eastern Shoshone and Northern Arapaho tribes. This book was originally written in the 1990s to illuminate the intricate workings of tribal government on this jointly shared land, which encompasses approximately two and a half million acres. Its purpose is to foster a deeper understanding of tribal governance, thereby enhancing problem-solving initiatives both within the tribes and in collaboration with the state of Wyoming. After nearly three decades, it was past time for a new edition to bring the content up to date with new laws and governmental changes.

This endeavor would not have been possible without the remarkable contributions of dedicated individuals who have passionately committed their time and expertise to this project.

The original publication was written by Janet Flynn. Her willingness to dive into this task to research and write it during the 1990s are foundational to bringing the history and functions of tribal governance to life in this book. Her initial vision and dedication ensured that the voices of the Eastern Shoshone and Northern Arapaho resonate throughout these pages.

We were also fortunate to have the support of Patti Trautman as we originally assembled and distributed this publication. She took the time to provide valuable updates to the tribal council appendices and her insights helped ensure that the material remained relevant and reflective of the contemporary landscape of tribal governance during the first years after its publication.

She, and her company Mortimore Publishing, kept the publication in print for many years.

However, by 2014, it was clear that so much had changed that we needed to significantly edit the booklet. I approached the Wyoming Humanities Council (now known as Wyoming Humanities) to seek support in creating a new edition. I thank the Executive Director at that time, Shannon Smith, who soon joined me to raise funds and find content experts to update the book.

This project quickly became more extensive than we planned and it seemed like we would never find the right team to edit and write this much-needed new edition. Then, we enlisted Katie Swistowicz and Clint Wagon to refine the content of this book. Their observations and suggestions made it possible for us to gain a clearer vision of what we needed to do to provide a comprehensive description of the contemporary workings of the tribal council, including the latest information on elections and an overview of court systems.They also advised we needed to include insights into gaming laws and their implications, an increasingly important cross-section of tribal sovereignty and economic development. We agreed that this warranted a whole new chapter and we are grateful for the hard work Andy Baldwin, an attorney from Lander with deep knowledge of tribal gaming law, put into this new chapter.

After retiring from Wyoming Humanities, Shannon Smith took the lead in pushing this book project through to completion. She viewed the book in its entirety and negotiated with both Wyoming Humanities and WyoHistory.org for permission to add "Two Nations, One Reservation," based upon their joint project of the same name, as a new chapter to tell the complex story of how these two tribes came to reside on the same reservation. She edited all of the chapters and added brief bibliographies to each as suggestions for further reading. She also brought WyoHistory—Wyoming's online encyclopedia—into the project, including Editor Kylie McCormick and Editor Emeritus Tom Rea. WyoHistory will assume the rights for the book in order to keep it updated during the coming years as the inevitable changes to laws, policies, and regulations impact tribal governance on the Wind River Reservation.

It has been my honor to witness this book evolve over several decades into a vital resource for citizens and students alike, all of whom seek to understand how tribal governance operates. As you delve into these pages, I encourage you to engage with the stories and information presented herein—may they foster a greater respect for the rich heritage and ongoing contributions of the Eastern Shoshone and Northern Arapaho tribes.

Together, let us celebrate the spirit of collaboration and education that this book embodies, paving the way for continued and future dialogues and partnerships between the Eastern Shoshone and Northern Arapaho tribe in the State of Wyoming.

— *Scotty Ratliff*

INTRODUCTION

This book is not intended as a definitive statement on the nature and status of tribal government. Rather, it is a beginning explication of the government of the Eastern Shoshone and Northern Arapaho tribes on the Wind River Indian Reservation, written to promote a better understanding of the full scope and variety of modem government in the state of Wyoming. Though it is primarily intended for Wyoming students of government, it may be useful as a comparative tool in a variety of other settings.

It arose from a need for a better understanding of how tribal government functions, not just in isolation, but also in interaction with local, state, and federal governments. Research into the structure and process of government at Wind River by its nature involved examination of the enigmatic web of Native American culture, which is necessarily reflected in the text at times. But tribal culture is not the primary focus of the book, and apologies are made in advance for incomplete and imperfect renderings of the culture of the two tribes at Wind River.

Also, the biases of historical record and previous chroniclers of reservation life are sometimes evident in the text. The history and early development of tribal government at Wind River is far from concrete. Unfortunately, little has been written from which to piece together a potentially more objective picture. Even such fundamental and long ago things as the treaties establishing the Wind River Reservation are interpreted in significantly disparate ways yet today. Perhaps the only way to avoid such pitfalls is to have been there, or to talk at length with those who were, which, unfortunately, was seldom possible. The goal, of course, is to keep moving closer to understanding both government and culture at Wind River with each successive step.

This book will be helpful for teachers and students of Wyoming government as a supplement to their primary Federal and state source books. As the world grows more interconnected politically, socially, and economically, it becomes increasingly important to understand and respect the diversity of our social systems, our cultures, and our neighbors.

Many people contributed to the book in critical ways. I would like to thank especially my partner in the project, Scott Ratliff, who served as a crucial liaison to the tribes throughout the project. Thanks also to all who were helpful in reviewing preliminary drafts of the test and to Central Wyoming College, NOWCAP, and the State Department of Education, who backed the project directly or through loans of equipment, staff, and other support. Finally, I am indebted to all of the people who consented to be interviewed or provided information for the book, including members of the Shoshone and Arapaho Business Council and Judiciary, as well as the staff at the Wind River Bureau of Indian Affairs.

— *Janet Flynn*

ACKNOWLEDGEMENTS

This edition of *Tribal Government: Wind River Reservation* is a testament to the value of tenacity. The effort and dedication of Scott Ratliff, who spent well over a decade putting the right people and resources together to get a new edition of this book published, has been a wonder to behold. After the first two printings of the book were done in 1991 and 1998, it has essentially been out of print. But Scott was constantly being asked where people could get a copy. In 2018, when he came to the Wyoming Humanities Council with a proposal to republish the book, we wanted to have a copy for ourselves and discovered only three copies for sale anywhere online. We ended up buying the least expensive one on eBay for $25 (seven years later, we could find only one copy available for $90). We knew it was an important resource and it fit the mission of our organization, especially our commitment to using the humanities in support of Native American history and culture, so we raised the funding necessary to publish a new version. Little did I know what a journey this project would turn out to be.

Scott describes the writing, publishing, and distribution of this book's early editions in the following foreword. Janet Flynn is the original author, and Scott oversaw raising funds, publishing, and printing of the book, first with Lauren Jost of Big Bend Press in 1991 and then with Patti Trautman of Mortimore Publishing in 1998. When he brought the project to me and the Wyoming Humanities Council in 2018, we thought it would be a straightforward project to quickly update the last chapters with the latest information about the structure and operations of the tribal government on the reservation. It turned out to be a much bigger project than we expected, though we should have realized just how much has changed on the reservation in the previous twenty years. Several people took a stab at the project, but it wasn't until 2022, when we asked Kate Swistowisz and Clint Wagon to take a deep dive into the content, that we realized just how much had changed structurally in Wind River tribal government since the 1990s and how much more needed to be said. By mid-2024, we recruited attorney Andy Baldwin, an expert on Indian Gaming Law, to review the entire contents of the book and write the story of bringing legal gaming to the Wind River Reservation. His work put us over the finish line. Now it was time to find a new publisher and get the book printed.

However, in early 2025, funding from the National Endowment for the Humanities to the State Humanities Councils was eliminated, and suddenly, Wyoming Humanities was facing a crisis. Through the determined leadership of their board of directors, first under President Maggi Murdock and then Stacy Stebner, and their newly-appointed Executive Director, Chloe Flagg, this project was funded to its completion. Next, we had to decide where to assign the future republishing rights. We want this to be a "living" book–to be updated as major issues in Native American sovereignty and legal processes impact tribal governmental operations. For that to happen, we wanted to assign the rights to an entity that would continuously monitor the historical narrative of Wind River Tribal Governance.

We found the perfect partner to assume that role. WyoHistory.org, founded in 2011, is our state's permanent, interactive online encyclopedia, and the primary source of online information about Wyoming history for the public, including teachers, students, tourists, public officials, history enthusiasts, and scholars. WyoHistory.org also seeks readers' feedback as it continues to add high-quality articles and information about local resources, activities, and events–with significant content supporting the 2017 Indian Education for All standards developed by the state department of education. A perfect fit, indeed. We approached founding editor emeritus, Tom Rea, and the current editor, Kylie McCormick, who enthusiastically agreed to continue to curate the book and develop curricular materials.

WyoHistory recruited outside readers with expertise in Wyoming's Native American Education for All standards to review the book, including Iva Moss-Redman and Lynette St. Clair to whom we owe great thanks for their comments and helpful suggestions. They also brought in Renée Tafoya, Publisher at WordsWorth Publishing, to become the publisher of record for this new edition.

Last, but not least, we want to acknowledge Jon Cox, nationally renowned artist from Riverton, who graciously granted us a license to use his evocative painting, *Buffalo Spirits*; when Scott saw this painting, he knew it had to be the cover of our book.

I am grateful to have been able to work with all of these people to bring *Tribal Government: Wind River Reservation* back into print. It has been a labor of love. Thank you, Scotty, for bringing me on this journey.

— *Shannon D. Smith, Smithstorian Consulting, LLC*

NOTE FROM THE EDITORS

This book tells the evolution of tribal government on a reservation. It is a history deeply entangled with the legacies of colonialism, conquest, and federal oversight, and it cannot be told without using terms and frameworks that emerged from those contexts. Words such as reservation, sovereignty, wardship, allotment, and even tribal government are themselves products of a colonial legal and political order. They often fail to capture the depth and diversity of Indigenous governance traditions, and at times they obscure as much as they reveal.

As editors, we recognize that the very act of describing tribal government through the lens of U.S. law, federal policy, and court decisions inevitably re-centers colonial language. Yet, these frameworks remain unavoidable for understanding the historical and legal conditions under which Native nations have been forced to operate and against which they have asserted their sovereignty. Our aim is not to legitimize those structures but to critically trace their impact while also highlighting the enduring strength, adaptation, and self-determination of Native communities.

Readers should approach this work with an awareness of this tension. Where possible, we have sought to foreground Indigenous perspectives and to acknowledge the limits of colonial terminology. We invite readers to read critically, to hold space for the complexity of language, and to honor the many ways Native nations have sustained governance practices that predate and transcend colonial impositions.

Throughout the text, readers will see the Wind River nations referenced as "Eastern Shoshone", "Shoshone", "Northern Arapaho", and "Arapaho." At the time of publication, the U.S. federal government officially recognizes each nation as "Eastern Shoshone Tribe of the Wind River Reservation, Wyoming [previously listed as Shoshone Tribe of the Wind River Reservation, Wyoming]" and "Arapaho Tribe of the Wind River Reservation, Wyoming." The Wind River nations refer to themselves as, "Eastern Shoshone Tribe" and the "Northern Arapaho Tribe of Wyoming."

Chapter 1

EARLY GOVERNMENT AND TRIBAL HISTORY

A COMPARATIVE VIEW

Many American Indian tribes had complicated systems of government long before the European invasion and subsequent colonization of North America. Often, colonists did not believe that people they encountered had any government system at all—that indigenous Americans were living in relative anarchy, without the European-based rules and regulations to which the colonists were accustomed.[1] Some observers in Colonial America viewed the Indians enviously because of this apparent absence of formal European government, and others thought it was proof of their primitive way.

In truth, however, the colonists frequently did not understand the traditional governments of the American Indian Tribes, many of which were well-developed and quite complex. Early settlers simply were unfamiliar with what the Indian government was, especially given language barriers and the fact that few written documents of the Indian government existed.

The traditional government of the Iroquois, the Great Binding Law of the Five Nations, was the first written constitution drafted in North America, predating the arrival of Columbus in 1492. Written on sacred wampum belts, it included such democratic notions as voting, recall, and referendum. Scholars suggest that Benjamin Franklin and other founders of the U.S.

---

1   Vine Deloria, Jr. and Clifford M. Lytle, *American Indians, American Justice.* (Austin: University of Texas Press, 1983), 81.

constitutional democracy noted the structure that made up the Iroquois government as they constructed the U.S. Constitution.[2]

KEY NAMES AND TERMS
• Great Binding Law of the Five Nations
• Age grading
• Consensus
• Headmen
• Chief Washakie
• Chief Sharpnose
• Chief Black Coal

Most tribal groups, however, did not have written forms of government, depending instead on stories, legends, and oral histories to express rules and political philosophies. Social pressure and the need for acceptance in the tribe were used to guide behavior. Good relations among extended family groups were highly valued.

Many practices of today's tribal governments can be traced to these group norms for behavior. Peacemaker Codes, used in some tribal courts for example, place heavy emphasis on maintenance of family and tribal harmony, reflecting traditional Native American norms for justice.

The place of religion in government of the tribes was often key, with tribal spiritual leaders and elders determining many of the tribes' decisions and activities. In fact, many Indian tribes were categorized as theocracies, centering their social and political life around religious laws and calendars.[3]

Also, tribes differed greatly in the forms of government they employed. Some tribes were much more structured and rigid in their forms of government than others, depending in large part upon their lifestyles and geographic location. Nomadic tribes like the Shoshones of the western plains and Rocky Mountains were much more loosely organized and flexible in government systems than the Iroquois. A rigid system of government would not have

---

2   Felix Cohen, *Handbook of Federal Indian Law*. (Albuquerque: University of New Mexico Press, 1942), 127–8.
3   Deloria & Lytle, 83.

been practical in the widely dispersed, relatively independent hunting and food-gathering bands of the Shoshones, who came into contact with one another less frequently and covered a far broader geographical territory than many eastern tribes.

One tribe with a very complex system of government were the Cheyenne. A huge council of 44 chiefs, including some military chiefs and some civilian chiefs, governed the tribe. They had formal rules for selection and replacement of these chiefs, and the job duties of each type were clearly delineated.[4] Many other tribes had similar council forms, predating the federal government's formation of today's tribal councils through the Bureau of Indian Affairs (BIA).

In almost every Indian tribe, the role of the chiefs and/ or councils was not to set policy and issue unilateral orders, as might be presumed from cultural stereotypes of the executive role in government, but to mediate between tribal members and to maintain the well-being of the tribe through bargaining and conflict resolution. The chiefs more often reflected tribal policy than set it, sometimes making considerable personal sacrifices to preserve tribal unity. The traditional system of settlement of crimes, through negotiations conducted by tribal leaders with the families involved, is still evident in many modern tribal judicial systems. Chiefs and councils were also involved in inter-tribal decision making about trade and warfare, as well as the formation of alliances among various tribes. On the whole, early tribal government was more consensus based than the judicial, legislative, or executive structures we are familiar with in the United States.

---

4   Leo A. Killsback, *A Sovereign People: Indigenous Nationhood, Traditional Law, and the Covenants of the Cheyenne Nation*. (Lubbock: Texas Tech University Press, 2019), 77.

THE WIND RIVER TRIBES
THE ARAPAHOS

The tribe known as the Arapaho migrated through millions of acres across the plains of the United States. The Great Lakes area, Arkansas, Nebraska, Kansas, Iowa, South Dakota, Colorado, Wyoming, Montana, and Utah are considered homelands for the Arapaho tribe. The Northern Arapaho, one of the two tribes on the Wind River Reservation, is the main tribe of Arapaho, from whom the Southern Arapaho and Gros Ventre tribes are derived. The first colonial recorded history placed them in the area of northern Minnesota, close to what is now the Canadian border. Several hundred years ago, probably during the 1600s, the tribe migrated south and west. By the mid–1800s, the Northern and Southern Arapaho had split into two distinct groups. The northern branch of this group was spread out through parts of Nebraska, Kansas, Iowa, Wyoming, South Dakota, and Colorado by the 1800s. Their homeland was centered in what is now the greater Denver area and Northern Colorado has many place names reflecting their connection including Arapahoe County, Left Hand, Niwot, and many other Arapaho-based names.

Within the Arapaho tribe were several bands. Though membership in the bands was usually determined by birth and geography, movement from membership in one band to membership in another was flexible and freely allowed among these people.

Originally, there were four bands of Arapaho:[5] The Long Leg or Antelope band, the Greasy Face band, the Quick-to-Anger band, and the Beaver Band.

Age-grading, or the custom of allotting status and power in

---

5   *Social Studies: History, Customs and Culture of Wyoming's Indian Tribes*, (Wyoming State Department of Education Curriculum Workshop, 1972); C. W. Buchholtz, *Rocky Mountain National Park: A History*, (Denver: University Press of Colorado, 1987), Chapter 1.

KEY NAMES AND TERMS

ARAPAHO
Algonquian-Wahashan
Linguistic Family

Related Tribes
• Cree
• Blood
• Blackfoot
• Piegan
• Gros Ventre
• Cheyenne

Early Arapaho Bands
*(before geographical
redistribution)*

• Long Leg (Antelope)
• Quick-to-Anger
• Greasy Face
• Beaver

SHOSHONE
Uto-Aztecan Linguistic Family

Related Tribes
• Bannock
• Ute
• Chemehuevi
• Panamint
• Comanche
• Paiute
• Snake

Shoshone Societies
• Yellow Noses
• Logs
• Women and Children

*Source: Wyoming State Department of
Education Curriculum Workbook, 1972*

the tribe based upon achievement of particular age categories, was an important part of Arapaho politics and social life. The Arapaho believed that childhood and youth, the first and second stages of life, could last as long as 40 years, until a person demonstrated adequate wisdom and status in the tribe.

There were seven men's ceremonial lodges, each one representing attainment of higher status in the tribe. Tribal chiefs were usually selected from men in the later lodges, such as the sixth level, or Dog Lodge. These men, who were generally in their late forties and fifties, were in the "third hill of life", according to Arapaho age-grading. The highest status and authority was reserved for the oldest men and women in the tribe, who were the ceremonial leaders. They were authorized to perform religious and ceremonial rituals for the tribe. These included the Seven Water Pouring Old Men. They helped the tribe achieve cohesion through the performance of Offerings Lodge and other rituals, serving as intermediaries between the Creator and the Arapaho people.

Women had active roles in Arapaho life and were chosen

to conduct ceremonies and rituals on behalf of the welfare of individuals or families. Unfortunately, little is written about their specific roles in tribal government, though it is certain that both men and women elders were influential in shaping tribal conduct.[6]

Age-grading and other ceremonial rites among the Arapaho were important symbolic rituals which defined and legitimized authority, bringing order to Arapaho political life. These ceremonies and rituals augmented tribal government, providing an atmosphere of common purpose and value systems which emphasized decisions by consensus and respect for the wisdom of elders.

THE SHOSHONES

The Shoshone Indians, of which the Eastern Shoshone tribe on the Wind River Reservation is part, were at one time located in bands from the arid desert land of California, across Nevada, and into Utah, Idaho, and Wyoming. They were thought to be in the Rocky Mountain and Plains areas as early as the 1500s.[7] The Shoshones were relatively peaceful Indians until encroachment on their lands by other tribes and non-Indians forced them to compete for game and land. When they acquired horses and guns, they became a fearsome foe to encounter in battle. The Shoshones were noted for their superb horsemanship.

The Shoshone had a warrior society among the men of the tribe, called the Yellow Noses. They spoke "backwards", using inverted speech and moving ahead of the tribe, leaving the role of protecting the women and children, maintenance of the tribal lodges, and other daily functions to the other society of men, called

---

6   Loretta Fowler, *Arapaho Politics, 1851–1978: Symbols in Crises of Authority* (Lincoln: University of Nebraska Press, 1982), 109–11.
7   Virginia C. Trenholm and Maurine Carley, *The Shoshonis: Sentinels of the Rockies* (Lincoln: University of Nebraska Press, 1964), 17.

An Eastern Shoshone camp near South Pass in 1870, two years after the
Shoshone Reservation was established. Washakie's lodge is at the center.
William Henry Jackson photo, University of Wyoming American Heritage Center.

the Logs.[8] Membership in these societies was mostly formed as a result of friendship or kin ties, there being no specific requirements to prevent membership in either society. The Shoshones did not have formal age-grading categories like the Arapaho, but they also placed great stock in the wisdom of their elders.

The role of intermediary or middleman was present in Arapaho and Shoshone society before contact with settlers. Tribal government itself tended to be more fragmented and autonomous than today, originating in and scattered among the tribal bands or societies. Tribal middlemen, or "headmen" as they were called, acted as tribal representatives in trade and other negotiations among Plains tribes in times of war or major hunts. The arrival of European traders and, later, American colonial traders and government representatives reinforced the need for the tribes to have designated, centralized leaders.

In the mid–1800s, the U.S. government requested that the

---

8   Trenholm & Carley, 30.

tribes appoint official "chiefs" to act as spokesmen for the tribes in government to government negotiations. Subchiefs represented the various bands within the tribes. Chief Washakie of the Shoshone and Chiefs Black Coal and Sharp Nose of the Arapaho were three of the last chiefs of the Wind River tribes, representing the beginning of the transition from the chief system to the modern-day council.

CHIEF WASHAKIE OF THE SHOSHONES

Chief Washakie led the Shoshone tribe for 60 years, from the 1840s until his death in 1900. His name means Rawhide Rattle, derived from the buffalo-skin rattle, which he reportedly used to spook enemy horses in battle.[9] Washakie was known as a great statesman, orator, and friend of the U. S. government, serving at times as a scout for the U. S. Army. Indeed, when he died in 1900, he was buried with full military honors.[10]

By the 1860s, the Shoshones camped for much of each year in the Wind River Valley, which they called "Warm Valley." It was for this land that Washakie carefully negotiated in many treaty councils with the United States. Beginning with the first treaty of Fort Bridger, in 1863, the vast Shoshone lands were diminished from over 44 million acres, covering parts of Utah, Idaho, Montana, Wyoming, and Colorado, to the reservation's current size of 2.2 million acres. In all his dealings, Washakie would try to retain this "Warm Valley."

Washakie lived for over three decades on the reservation and served as its governmental leader through his whole life. He was a friend of Brigham Young, the second president of the Church of Jesus Christ of Latter-day Saints, and in 1880, Washakie and

---

9   Larry Murray, ed., *Wind River Reservation Yesterday and Today: The Legends, the Land, the People*, (Wind River Reservation Curriculum Development Workshop, 1972), 11.
10   *Wind River: The People and Places*, (Wyoming: North American Indian Heritage Center, St. Stephen's), 2.

Washakie, chief of the Eastern Shoshones, in 1870. William Henry Jackson photo, University of Wyoming American Heritage Center.

about three hundred other Shoshones accepted baptism into the Mormon church. A few years later, however, Washakie befriended the local Episcopal missionary, Father John Roberts, and over several decades, their friendship deepened as the Episcopal Church built multiple schools and churches on both the Shoshone and Arapaho sides of the reservation. Washakie was baptized by Roberts in 1897 and when the revered chief died three years later, on February 22, 1900, he was buried in the Episcopal cemetery at Fort Washakie in a service officiated by Father Roberts.

In spite of his generally cooperative orientation to dealings with the U. S. government, Washakie experienced frustration and disappointment with disingenuous and duplicitous actions of his federal counterparts over the years. Two very different attitudes of the great chief toward Shoshone relations with the government are illustrated in the speech below. The first was spoken by Chief Washakie in council following the signing of the 1868 treaty establishing the boundaries of the Wind River Reservation. He delivered the second comments ten years later to government officials regarding the same treaty:

1868

I am laughing because I am happy. Because my heart is good. As I said two days ago, I like the country you mentioned, then, for us, the Wind River valley. Now I see my friends are around me, and it is pleasant to meet and shake hands with them. I always find friends along the roads in this country, about Bridger, that is why I come here. It is good to have the Railroad through this country and I have come down to see it.

When we want to grow something to eat and hunt, I want the Wind River Country. In other Indian countries, there is danger, here it is safe for all to travel. When the white man came into my country and cut the wood and made the roads, my heart was good, and I was satisfied. You have heard what I want. The Wind River Country is the one for me.

We may not for one, two, or three years be able to till the ground. The Sioux may trouble us. But when the Sioux are taken care of, we can do well. Will the whites be allowed to build houses on our reservation? I do not object to traders coming among us, and care nothing about the miners and mining country where they are getting out gold. I may, bye and bye, get some of that myself.

I want for my home the valley of the Wind River and lands on its tributaries as far east as the Popo-Agie and want the privilege of going over the mountains to hunt where I please.[11]

---

11   Gen. C. C. Augur (1868), quoted in Trenholm & Carley, p. 22.

1878

The white man's government promised that if we, the Shoshones, would be content with the little patch allowed us, it would keep us well supplied with everything necessary to comfortable living, and would see that no white man would cross our borders for our game, or for anything that is ours. But it has not kept its word!

The white man kills our game, captures our furs, and sometimes feeds his herds upon our meadows. And your great and mighty government . . . does not protect our rights. It leaves us without the promised seed, without tools for cultivating the land, without implements for harvesting our crops, without breeding animals better than ours, without the food we still lack . . . without the many comforts we cannot produce, without the schools we so much need for our children.

I again say, the government does not keep its word, and so, after all we can get by cultivating the land, and by hunting and fishing, we are sometimes nearly starved, and go half naked, as you see us! Knowing all this, do you wonder, sir, that we have fits of desperation and think to be avenged? [12]

CHIEF BLACK COAL OF THE ARAPAHO

After the death of Chief Medicine Man in the winter of 1871–72, Black Coal became the principal chief of the Northern Arapaho tribe. As a young man, Black Coal was a distinguished warrior. He served as scout for the U. S. government, assisting the roundup of Sioux and Northern Cheyenne by General Crook and his forces in 1876. In return, Crook promised Black Coal a reservation for his people

---

12   J. W. Hoyt to Secretary of Interior, quoted in Trenholm & Carley, p. 280.

near the Tongue River in Northern Wyoming. This promise, unfortunately, lasted only as long as General Crook was alive. A reservation at Tongue River was never granted to the Arapaho. In 1878, Black Coal's camp, along with many other Arapahos, settled into the Wind River Reservation.

In addition to his accomplishments as a warrior and government scout, Black Coal is remembered for his role in helping to bring education to the reservation. His donations of land and assistance helped found St. Stephen's Catholic

Black Coal. University of Wyoming American Heritage Center.

Mission, the largest of three missions established at Wind River. In addition to a boarding school and church, the mission included a farm, cattle ranch, and a dairy herd to support the mission staff and tribal students. Black Coal worked hard to encourage education among the young people of his tribe until his death in 1893.

CHIEF SHARPNOSE OF THE ARAPAHO

Born in 1830, Sharpnose rose through the ranks of Arapaho leadership, becoming first a chief of the most feared warrior society called the Bad Pipe Clan-Dog Soldiers.[13]

One of his greatest accomplishments was in preventing the U.S. government from moving the Northern Arapaho to Oklahoma. Instead, he was able to convince government

---

13   Murray, 11.

Sharp Nose, in the uniform indicating his service as a U.S. Army scout in 1876. University of Wyoming American Heritage Center.

officials to let his tribe stay in their home territory, eventually settling on Wind River Reservation, where they remain.[14]

Sharpnose died in 1901, one year after the death of Chief Washakie. His last words, as reported by Charles Little Ant, were: "My friend, I am dying of my battle wounds. Watch out for our children and yourselves, stay together, as the Arapaho have always been together since the beginning—beware of the stranger and his strange ways."

SUMMARY

Tribal nations in North America varied significantly in the form and complexity of their governments, and continue to today. Traditional ways of governing depended in part on geographic location in addition to cultural and other factors. It has been observed that those reservations that had powerful and prestigious chiefs residing therein resisted more successfully and longer the intrusion of non-Indian methods into tribal governance.[15]

Age-grading customs of tribes like the Northern Arapaho helped to create bonds among different age groups within the tribe, as well as among men from different families. This custom enhanced the unity of the tribe and helped ease tension and reduce conflict in tribal decision-making and political processes.

---

14   Murray, 12.
15   Deloria, 97.

A dramatic change among Plains tribes like the Eastern Shoshones was the location of all tribal members in one place. The establishment of the Wind River Reservation permanently altered the structure of tribal government. Before reservation life, the individual bands governed themselves and roamed independently, except on rare occasions, when a council-like form of government was employed for undertakings of the tribe which required the cooperation of all. Then, individual band leaders met jointly and functioned as chiefs in directing communal activities such as hunting or warring. To suddenly have all the bands under common governance was a major adjustment for early chiefs and council members on the reservation. The political body of the Eastern Shoshone tribe went from bands of 100 to 200 people conducting their own affairs to more than 1,000 members attempting to govern together. This represented a shift from local to federal government, and the tribes took on the character of a national government.

Also, confinement to a particular piece of land brought new types of needs and political questions to the tribal members, who suddenly had to adjust their concepts of land use and ownership in ways never before required. As will be seen in later chapters, much of tribal government during early reservation days centered around use and ownership of the land. In fact, land use and ownership continues to this day to be a real political issue on the Wind River Reservation and many other reservations nationwide.

For Further Reading:

NORTHERN CHEYENNE (SELECTED BOOKS)

Killsback, Leo K. *A Sacred People: Indigenous Governance, Traditional Leadership, and the Warriors of the Cheyenne Nation.* Volume 1 of 2. Texas Tech University Press, 2020. Killsback, a citizen of the Northern Cheyenne Nation, reconstructs and rekindles an ancient Cheyenne world—ways of living and thinking that became casualties of colonization and forced assimilation. Spanning more than a millennium of antiquity and recovering stories and ideas interpreted from a Cheyenne worldview, the works' joint purpose is rooted as much in a decolonization roadmap as it is in preservation of culture and identity for the next generations of Cheyenne people. Dividing the story of the Cheyenne Nation into pre- and post-contact, A Sacred People and A Sovereign People lay out indigenously conceived possibilities for employing traditional worldviews to replace unhealthy and dysfunctional ones bred of territorial, cultural, and psychological colonization.

Grinnell, George Bird. *The Cheyenne Indians: Their History and Ways of Life.* 2 vols., originally 1923; reissued by University of Nebraska Press/Bison, 1972. Foundational ethnographic history of Cheyenne society and traditions.

Sandoz, Mari. *Cheyenne Autumn.* University of Nebraska Press/Bison, 2005. Narrative history of the 1878–79 Northern Cheyenne exodus; central to the literature.

Stands In Timber, John, and Margot Liberty. *Cheyenne Memories.* Yale University Press/Bison, 1998. Classic oral history spanning pre-reservation to early reservation years.

Stands In Timber, John; edited by Margot Liberty. *A Cheyenne Voice: The Complete John Stands In Timber Interviews.* University of Oklahoma Press, 2019. Full interview corpus behind Cheyenne Memories; invaluable primary source.

Marquis, Thomas B. *Wooden Leg: A Warrior Who Fought Custer.* various
Bison/University of Nebraska Press editions. First-person Northern
Cheyenne perspective on the 1876 war and lifeways.

Liberty, Margot (ed.). *A Northern Cheyenne Album: Photographs
by Thomas B. Marquis.* University of Oklahoma Press, 2007. Early
reservation-era photographs with interpretive captions.

Leiker, James N., and Ramon Powers. *The Northern Cheyenne Exodus
in History and Memory.* University of Oklahoma Press, 2011.
Historiography and memory studies of the exodus narrative.

EASTERN SHOSHONE (SELECTED BOOKS)

Stamm IV, Henry E. *People of the Wind River: The Eastern Shoshones,
1825–1900.* University of Oklahoma Press, 1999. The go-to political and
social history through the reservation's early decades. (Also listed under
Wind River.)

Hebard, Grace Raymond. *Washakie: Chief of the Shoshones.* originally
1930; University of Nebraska Press reprint. Influential early biography of
Washakie; widely cited (read with modern critiques in mind).

Madsen, Brigham D. *The Shoshoni Frontier and the Bear River Massacre.*
University of Utah Press, 1985. Essential background on Shoshone-U.S.
conflict leading up to the reservation era.

Madsen, Brigham D. *The Northern Shoshoni.* Caxton Printers, 1980.
Ethnohistory of Shoshone groups (especially Idaho/Utah) illuminating
broader Shoshone history.

Chapter 2

TWO NATIONS, ONE RESERVATION

In the spring of 1878, about 950 Northern Arapaho people arrived with an Army escort on the Shoshone Indian Reservation in the Wind River Valley in central Wyoming Territory. The two tribes had been in open warfare as recently as four years before, and bad feelings lingered between them.

Ten years earlier, in 1868, the U.S. government had promised the Northern Arapaho a reservation of their own. Some Northern Arapaho at that time had agreed, reluctantly, that they might be willing to settle in one of three places: on the Missouri River with the Lakota Sioux, on the Yellowstone with the Crow or in Indian Territory—present Oklahoma—with their southern Cheyenne and Arapaho relatives.

Neither locating with their one-time enemies, the Crow, nor with the Lakota, who were much more numerous and powerful,

KEY NAMES AND TERMS	
Fort Laramie Treaty of 1851 (Horse Creek Treaty)	Governor John Campbell
	Washakie (Eastern Shoshone)
Friday (Arapaho leader and interpreter)	Black Bear (Northern Arapaho)
Sand Creek Massacre of 1864	Medicine Man (Northern Arapaho)
Bozeman Trail	The Brunot Cession
Red Cloud's War	Black Coal (Northern Arapaho)
Treaty of Fort Laramie of 1868	Sharpnose (Northern Arapaho)
Transcontinental railroad	Red Cloud Agency
Fort Bridger Treaty of 1863	Bates Battle on Trout Creek
South Pass	

held much attraction for the Arapaho, however. And Indian Territory was hot, flat and too far from the country of the northern plains and mountains that the Northern Arapaho knew best. Traders since earliest times, they had always moved about more than many other Plains tribes. In the years after the Treaty of Fort Laramie of 1868, they kept moving, while the Army and the government, busy with other questions, left the question of an Arapaho homeland unresolved.

It would remain unresolved for ten more years, until the government located the Northern Arapaho on a reservation guaranteed earlier exclusively to the Shoshone. Members of both tribes still reside on the Wind River Reservation, as the reservation was officially renamed in the 1930s.

LIFE ON THE NORTHERN PLAINS

Ethnohistorians say the Arapaho people, under pressure from the north and east, moved out of northern plains and woodlands and crossed the Missouri River sometime in the mid-1700s, though Arapaho tradition places this event much earlier.

By 1806, white chroniclers recorded Arapaho people as far south as the Arkansas River in present southern Colorado; by the 18-teens, southern bands had congregated in that region, while northern Arapaho bands were ranging north from the mountain parks of Colorado, west of modern places like Fort Collins and Boulder. Northern Arapaho elders who live on the Wind River Reservation today say they still regard those parts of the northern Colorado plains and mountains as their spiritual and historic homeland.[1]

When Fort Laramie on the North Platte River and Bent's Fort on the Arkansas were established in the 1830s along the

---

1   "Arapaho elders ... say they still regard..." Crawford and Nelson White conversations with WyoHistory.org editor Tom Rea, Fort Washakie, Wyo., September, November 2017.

An Arapaho Village. Harper's Monthly magazine, March 1880. Wyoming State Archives

Rocky Mountain Front, Arapaho and Cheyenne people began trading at the forts. North-south divisions within the two tribes became more permanent: Northern Arapaho and Northern Cheyenne traded at Fort Laramie; Southern Arapaho and Southern Cheyenne traded at Bent's Fort, in what is now south-eastern Colorado.

In the 1840s, emigrant travel to Oregon, Utah and California swelled from a trickle to a flood. The Oregon Trail up the Platte, North Platte and Sweetwater rivers to the Continental Divide passed through the middle of northern Arapaho ranges and quickly began changing their lives. By the middle of the decade, it was already clear that emigrants and their livestock were to blame for the shrinking buffalo herds. Arapaho people told traveler and writer Lewis Garrard that "the white man was bad, that he ran the buffalo out of the country and starved the Arapahoes." As resources dwindled, conflict and warfare among the plains tribes rose sharply.

PROMINENT HISTORICAL THEMES
Written vs. oral – Tribes traditionally pass down history through oral traditions while Euro-Americans place more trust in the written word.
Horses & guns – Nomadic pedestrian native culture is changed by innovations that transform travel, hunting, war, and relationships with others.
Chasing gold & building railroads – The government steadily favors prospectors, railroad builders, and homesteaders over tribal interests.
Climate of fear & violence – In 1824, the Bureau of Indian Affairs is added to the War Department. Hostile attitudes toward Indians increase tensions as Euro-Americans move west.
Assigned lands – In 1818, a U.S. government official first mentions "colonies" for Indian tribes – separate places where natives would be taught farming and Christianity and be protected from the perceived vices of white people.
Broken treaties – Treaties with other nations, including Indian nations, must be ratified once negotiated. Between 1778 and 1871, the government signs more than 500 treaties with Indian nations. Most were poorly enforced, broken, or remained unratified

Then gold was discovered in California and trail traffic swelled by a factor of ten. With the buffalo more scattered, the tribes needed horses more than ever. Lakota, Cheyenne and Arapaho warriors began raiding the trails, especially for horses and mules.

Hoping to avoid conflict, yet at the same time aware the West was far too large to be militarily controlled, government officials decided it was time to make a treaty with the tribes of the northern plains.[2]

ARAPAHOS AND THE FORT LARAMIE TREATY OF 1851

In September 1851, about 10,000 Indians gathered near Fort

---

2   Loretta Fowler, *Arapaho Politics, 1851-1978: Symbols in Crises of Authority*, (Lincoln, Neb.: University of Nebraska Press, 1982), 15-24; "the white man was bad . . .", p. 23.

Laramie to negotiate. Under the treaty signed that month, the tribes of the northern plains would allow the United States to establish Army posts and make roads through Indian territory. They also agreed to the government's proposal to assign specific lands to specific tribes, as shown on a map drawn at the time by the Jesuit Catholic missionary Father Pierre-Jean De Smet. Tribes were allowed to live and hunt wherever they liked—on their lands or others—as long as they remained peaceful.

Lands north of the Arkansas River, east of the Continental Divide and south of the North Platte River were assigned jointly to the Arapaho and Cheyenne. This included most of what is now eastern Colorado plus large parts of southeastern Wyoming, western Nebraska and western Kansas.

In return, the government promised the tribes annual payments of $50,000 in goods, for 50 years. The U.S. Senate ratified the treaty in 1852, the year following the signing, but with an important amendment. The payments—annuities, they were called—would last only ten years, or 15 if the president chose to extend the term.[3]

Already, that is, the government seemed not to be taking the treaty seriously. War broke out between the Army and the Lakota just three years later.

A GOLD STRIKE

In 1858, prospectors found gold near what is now Denver, right in the middle of the lands allocated to the Arapaho and Cheyenne by the Fort Laramie treaty. Within three years, 100,000 or more gold seekers and other whites poured into what soon became Colorado Territory. Along the trails, conflict grew and intensified.

This influx of newcomers widened the old geographical

---

3   Lesley Wischmann, "Separate Lands for Separate Tribes: The Fort Laramie Treaty of 1851," *WyoHistory.org*; "Treaty of Fort Laramie with the Sioux, etc." *Indian Affairs: Laws and Treaties*, Charles J. Kappler, editor. Vol. 2, Treaties. (Washington: Government Printing Office, 1904), 594-596.

divisions between northern and southern bands of Arapaho and Cheyenne people. Northern bands moved from the Colorado Front Range to the plains north of the North Platte River. Others stayed south, toward the Arkansas.

A TREATY FOR THE SOUTHERN CHEYENNE AND ARAPAHO

In 1861, representatives of some of the southern bands signed a treaty at Fort Wise on the Arkansas ceding all the land promised them in 1851 in exchange for a small reservation between the Arkansas and a nearby tributary, Sand Creek. Many other Cheyenne and Arapaho people complained at the time that only a minority of chiefs had signed, however, and that many of them did not understand what they were signing. No Northern Arapaho chiefs signed the treaty.[4]

SAND CREEK, MORE RAIDS AND AN ARMY CAMPAIGN

Late in 1864, Colorado troops massacred around 200 people, most of them women and children, in a peaceful Cheyenne and Arapaho village on Sand Creek. Shocked and angry, Cheyenne, Arapaho and Lakota people began making war in earnest along the trails.

In the winter and spring of 1865, southern bands moved north to the Powder River Basin of what's now Wyoming and Montana, still rich in buffalo. That July they attacked the Army post at Platte Bridge on the North Platte River; two dozen soldiers were killed that day.

By this time, there were three main bands of what would become known as the Northern Arapaho. Friday, a leader who had learned English in his youth, led an Arapaho band in the

---

4   Michael D. Troyer. "Treaty of Fort Wise," *Colorado Encyclopedia*. Accessed Nov. 25, 2017, at https://coloradoencyclopedia.org/article/treaty-fort-wise.

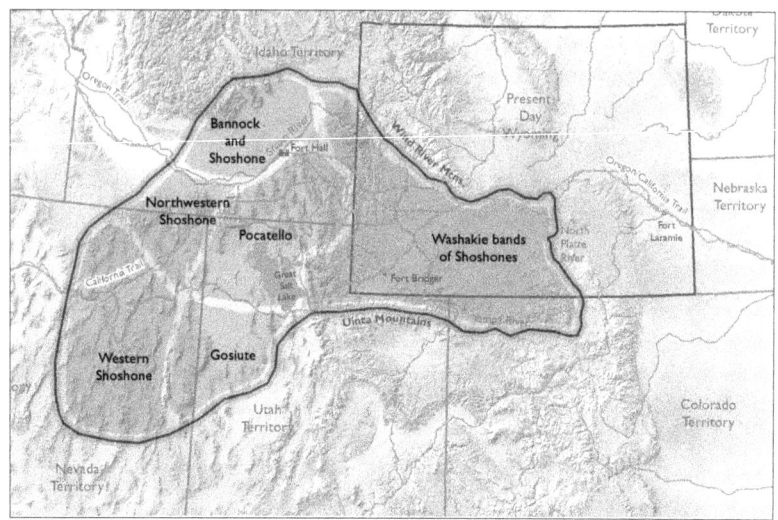

Shoshone territories as defined in the Fort Bridger Treaty of 1863,
Wyoming Geographic Information Science Center, University of Wyoming.

Cache la Poudre country around what is now Fort Collins, in northern Colorado. Medicine Man was a longtime leader of a group on the North Platte and Sweetwater ranges, where buffalo hunting was good. His group sometimes came into conflict with Eastern Shoshone bands. Arapaho people led by Black Bear married frequently among the Lakota and ranged in the Powder River Basin, from the North Platte to the Bighorns and east to the Black Hills. As hostilities increased, most of Friday's people joined the other two bands.[5]

In August 1865 the Army mounted a large campaign; one brigade attacked Black Bear's band in a village in the Powder River Country. The attack devastated the Northern Arapaho. They were a small tribe of only 180 lodges—perhaps 1,100 people in all the bands combined, at a time when smallpox and cholera were also spreading among them. After the attack, the Northern

---

5   Fowler, 43.

Arapaho could no longer raise large war parties.[6]

RED CLOUD'S WAR AND A SECOND FORT LARAMIE TREATY

Warfare continued to increase, especially along the Bozeman Trail, a new route from the Oregon Trail through the Powder River Basin to gold fields in Montana. The troubles came to be called Red Cloud's war, after the Oglala Lakota war leader; Capt. William Fetterman and his 80-man command were all killed in December 1866. Another fight nearby ended in a draw the following summer.

In the East, in the wake of the Sand Creek massacre and now the Fetterman fight, a peace faction had begun to emerge in Congress. The West, crisscrossed by stage lines, freight caravans, steamboat traffic on the Missouri and now a fast-building transcontinental railroad, was changing fast.

Early in 1868, government peace commissioners contacted the warring tribes. Commissioners paid Friday $315 to contact the Northern Arapaho bands with a clear ultimatum: Sign a treaty or there would be no more provisions.[7] On May 10, 1868, 150 lodges of Northern Cheyenne and Northern Arapaho met the commissioners at Fort Laramie to sign a treaty.

Signing for the Northern Arapaho were Medicine Man, Black Bear, Little Wolf, Littleshield and Sorrel Horse. Spotted Tail signed for the Brule Lakota, but no other important Lakota leaders signed that spring and summer. Finally, in November, the Oglala Lakota leaders signed the document as well.

A large reservation for the Lakota would be set aside on the west side of the Missouri River in Dakota Territory—the western half of present South Dakota—and the tribes, including the

---

6   Ellis Hein, "Connor's Powder River Expedition of 1865," *WyoHistory.org* accessed June 11, 2018, at /encyclopedia/connor's-powder-river-expedition-1865.
7   Fowler, 46.

U. S. Government treaty commissioners meeting with Cheyenne and Arapaho
negotiators at the Fort Laramie Treaty of 1868, National Archives.

Arapaho, could continue to hunt in the Powder River Basin.

The Arapaho agreed to settle within a year at one of three places: on the Missouri with the Lakotas, on the Yellowstone River in Montana Territory with the Crows or in Indian Territory—present Oklahoma—with their southern Cheyenne and Arapaho relatives.

This time, the government agreed to provide annuity goods for 30 years, plus schools, farm equipment and rations for Indians who settled permanently on the reservations.

But the Northern Arapaho, who disliked all three reservation alternatives offered them, continued to hope the government would find them a reservation of their own.[8]

_____

8   Fowler, 46-47; "Treaty with the Sioux, Brule, Oglala, Miniconjou, Yanktonai, Hunkpapa, Blackfeet, Cuthead, Two Kettle, Sans Arcs, and Santee, and Arapaho, 1868." *Indian Affairs: Laws and Treaties.* Charles J. Kappler, editor and compiler. Vol. II, Treaties, 1003-1006.

THE SHOSHONE RESERVATION

Also in the 1860s, the U.S. government negotiated two treaties with the Shoshone people that resulted in their coming to live in Warm Valley—the valley of the Big Wind River and its tributaries—in what is now west-central Wyoming.

The first treaty, signed in 1863, outlined a sprawling Shoshone homeland of around 44 million acres on both sides of the Continental Divide. (See map, p. 38) The second treaty, signed in 1868, shrank this to a far smaller reservation called the Shoshone Indian Reservation of around 3.2 million acres, with its heart in the Wind River Valley (See map, p. 42). The new reservation, according to the treaty, was established "for the absolute and undisturbed use and occupation of the Shoshone Indians herein named ..."

And in 1867, meanwhile, gold was discovered near South Pass, near the southern edge of what soon would become the reservation. Therefore, unlike most reservations, the Shoshone Indian Reservation on the Wind River had far more white people than native people living on it year-round at the time it was established. One historian estimates as many as 5,000 people lived in the gold-mining camps around South Pass and in the Wind River Valley 40 miles north, where whites were beginning to raise crops and livestock to feed the miners.[9]

Eastern Shoshone bands continued to live and hunt widely for another year or two before moving to the new reservation year-round.

In 1869, John Cambell, the new Wyoming Territory's first governor and Indian superintendent, arrived in Cheyenne. Gov. Campbell wanted the Shoshones to abandon their nomadic lives and settle on the new reservation.

Washakie, the leader of the Eastern Shoshones, was reluctant

---

9   Fowler, 48.

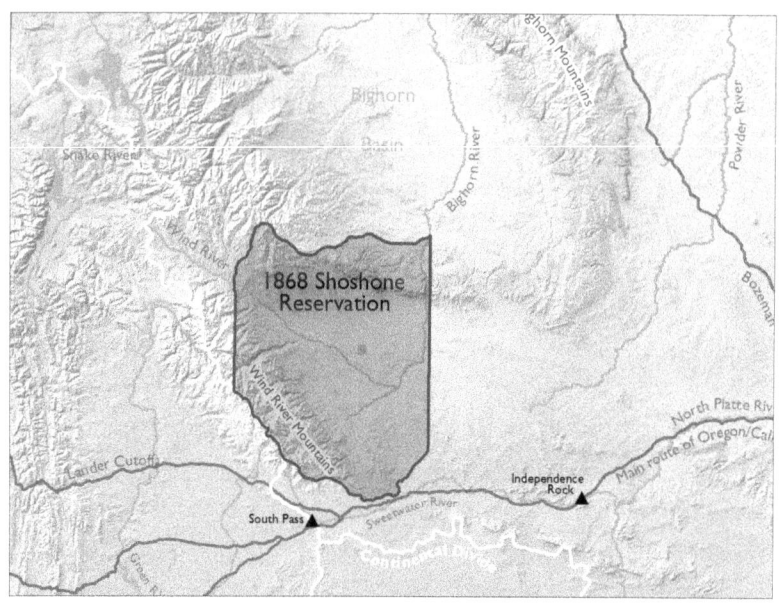

Boundaries of the Eastern Shoshone Indian Reservation, 1868,
Wyoming Geographic Information Science Center, University of Wyoming.

to move too quickly, however. He insisted the Eastern Shoshones be allowed to continue their old pattern of summers on Wind River and winters at Fort Bridger, where they could continue to receive their annuity goods.

ARAPAHOS HEAD TO WIND RIVER—THE FIRST TIME

Meanwhile, Northern Arapaho band leaders Medicine Man and Black Bear continued to press the government for a solution. They suggested a possible reservation on the North Platte River in Wyoming Territory near the old Platte Bridge, where an Army post had recently been abandoned. Government agents suggested they instead join their ethnic cousins the Gros Ventres on Milk River in northern Montana Territory. One hundred sixty lodges of Arapaho people spent the winter of 1868–1869 there, but a smallpox outbreak sent them on their way again in the spring.

The Arapaho chiefs had their eyes on Wind River Valley and

were hoping for some kind of accommodation with the Eastern Shoshone, their traditional enemies. Looking for a solution, Gov. Campbell and U.S. Army Gen. Christopher Augur set up a meeting for Washakie with Arapaho leaders Friday, Medicine Man and Sorrel Horse for October 1869.

A SKEPTICAL WASHAKIE

When the Arapahos arrived, however, Washakie was off hunting in the Bighorns, probably an indication of his doubts about Arapahos moving to the Shoshone Indian Reservation. Four months later, in February 1870, Arapaho leaders Medicine Man, Black Bear, Sorrel Horse, Little Wolf and Knock Knees came for a second meeting. This time, according to Arapaho tradition, the Shoshones agreed for the Arapahos to settle—temporarily—on the Shoshone Indian Reservation. Many Shoshones today say there was no such agreement at that time.

ARAPAHO ARRIVAL AND RETREAT

Northern Arapaho people began arriving in March. Soon, white settlers blamed them for Indian attacks that killed seven miners. On March 31 a mob of 250 white vigilantes, together with some Shoshones, attacked two groups of Arapaho moving from their camp on Wind River to trade in nearby Lander. About a dozen Arapahos were killed, including Black Bear.

Relations between the two tribes quickly deteriorated. The Arapaho began to leave. Medicine Man went to Fort Fetterman on the North Platte, and with the help of the trader and the post commander they convinced Territorial Gov. Campbell that Arapaho warriors had played no part in the recent attacks on the miners.[10]

The Eastern Shoshone, meanwhile, drew their annuity

---

10   Henry E. Stamm, IV, *People of the Wind River: The Eastern Shoshones, 1825-1900.* (Norman, Okla.: University of Oklahoma Press, 1999), 57; Fowler, 47-48.

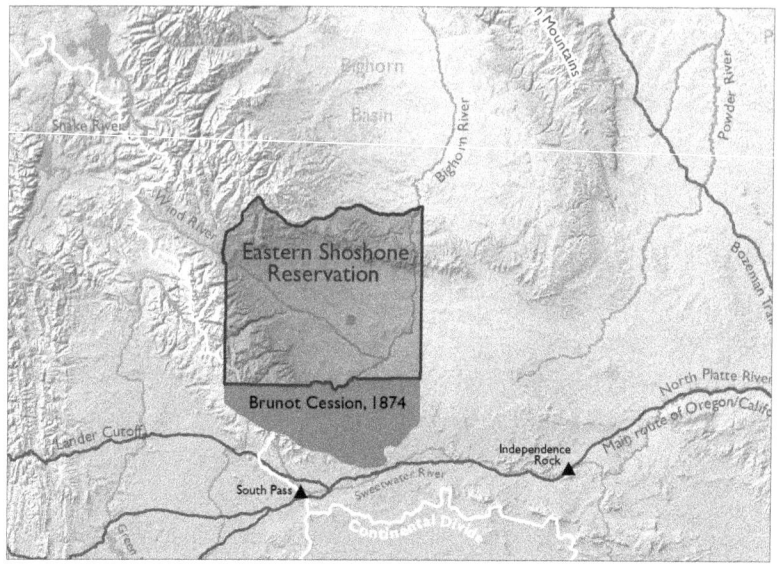

Shoshone Reservation, showing boundaries of the Brunot Cession, 1874

goods on the reservation for the first time that fall of 1870. Indian agents on the new reservation—the job turned over frequently— did little to curb the activities of the white miners, farmers and stock raisers who were now living illegally on Indian land.

THE BRUNOT CESSION

At the same time, the agents and Gov. Campbell began considering the idea of detaching the southern third or so of the reservation.

Under the terms of the Brunot Cession, negotiated in 1872 and ratified by Congress in 1874, the Eastern Shoshone tribe gave up around 700,000 acres—the valley of the Popo Agie River and areas around the town of Miner's Delight near South Pass. (See map, this page). In return, they received promises of $20,000 worth of cattle and $5,000 in cash, to be paid in annual installments over five years.

Cattle deliveries were slow in coming, however. And whites

began taking up land in the ceded portions long before Congress finalized the deal. The local white economy began growing away from mining toward farming and ranching. The gold mines were about played out anyway.[11]

NORTHERN ARAPAHO ON THE MOVE

By the winter of 1870-1871, the Northern Arapaho had left Wind River and were hunting in the Powder River Basin. Game was scarce, however. Chief Friday's band had joined the other Northern Arapahos by this time. With Friday as interpreter, the Arapaho leaders continued to cultivate friendships with Army officers, in hopes of winning their support for a new Arapaho reservation.

In March 1871, Arapaho Chiefs, Medicine Man, Friday, Littleshield and a new Arapaho leader named Black Coal agreed to draw their annuity goods with the Oglala Lakota at the Red Cloud Agency near Fort Laramie. But the Oglala treated them condescingly. The Arapaho stayed out in the Powder River country as much as possible, despite the dwindling buffalo supply.

A RAID ON TROUT CREEK

At the same time, Lakota, Cheyenne and most likely some Arapaho warriors continued, from time to time, to raid white and Shoshone people in the Wind River Valley. In 1872, a large raiding party attacked a Shoshone camp on Trout Creek, near the Indian agency. Shoshone scouts knew the raiders were coming, however, and sent the women and children up into the foothills of the Wind River Range to the west, for safety. Then they dug rifle pits inside their lodges, rolled up the bottom edges of their tipis and thus were able to fire out at the approaching raiders from solid defensive positions. The raiders were driven off. "We like to think we chased them all the way to Casper," meaning,

---

11   Stamm, 57-59, 64, 74-82, 92-95.

where Casper is now, 150 miles to the east, Shoshone elder John Washakie says.[12]

In the summer of 1874, in apparent reprisal for Arapaho raids, about 160 Shoshone warriors—30 of them enlisted as Army scouts—plus 60 cavalry troopers under Capt. Alfred E. Bates from Camp Brown on the Shoshone Indian Reservation attacked an Arapaho village on what has since been named Bates Creek, in the mountains between the Bighorn and Wind River basins. Arapaho men managed to gather at the top of a cliff, fire down on the attackers and drive them off. But many of the lodges were destroyed, 200 horses were stolen and, the Army estimated later, about 24 Arapaho people were killed.[13]

Though the soldiers and Shoshone warriors counted the fight a victory, by further impoverishing the Northern Arapaho the battle led to a series of events that ended up limiting Shoshone control over the lands the Fort Bridger Treaty had guaranteed them back in 1868.

THE LOSS OF THE BLACK HILLS

By this time, the buffalo supply was shrinking fast, the old ways of the tribes were steadily becoming more difficult to sustain and the U.S. government was turning up the pressure.

In the summer of 1874, Lt. Col. George A. Custer violated the 1868 Fort Laramie Treaty by leading an expedition of 1,000 troops through the Black Hills of Dakota and Wyoming territories. The troups found gold.

In 1875, the Oglala Lakotas relocated to a new Red Cloud Agency and the Brules to a new Spotted Tail Agency, both in northwestern Nebraska.

Northern Cheyenne and Northern Arapaho people, still

12   WyoHistory.org Editor Tom Rea conversation with John Washakie, March 2018.
13   Fowler, 50-52.

lacking an agency or reservation of their own, mingled with the Oglalas at Red Cloud Agency. Rations there were poor, the annuity flour was so bad the Indians sold it for horse feed and some Arapaho children starved to death. Arapahos near Fort Fetterman killed and ate their horses and begged at the post.[14]

The next year, the government began pressing the Lakota to sell the Black Hills. Among the Oglala, Red Cloud and others were ready to sign; Crazy Horse stayed out in the Powder River country and refused. In 1876, Army campaigns against the resisters resulted in the death of Custer and 267 of his men that June at the Little Bighorn.

Government officials began pressing even harder on the tribes at the Red Cloud Agency for sale of the Black Hills. All were reluctant, but again it came down to an ultimatum: Sign or starve. Together with the Lakota and the Northern Cheyenne, the Northern Arapaho signed a document in September giving up their claims to the Black Hills. With only 10% of the Lakota signing the agreement, the sale of the Black Hills was a clear violation of the 1868 Fort Laramie Treaty, which stated that any cession of lands in the Great Sioux Reservation must be agreed upon by 75% of the adult male Lakota population. On June 30, 1980, the U.S. Supreme Court recognized this violation and found in favor of the "Sioux Nation."

Facing starvation, the Arapaho in 1876 agreed to settle with the Lakota near Fort Randall on the Missouri River in southern Dakota Territory—or to head south to Indian Territory.[15]

SHOSHONE AND ARAPAHO SCOUTS IN THE GREAT SIOUX WAR

As the so-called Great Sioux War—of which Custer's campaign

---

14   Fowler, pp. 53-56; Robert M. Utley, *The Indian Frontier of the American West, 1846-1890*. (Albuquerque: University of New Mexico Press, 2003), 174.
15   Fowler, 56-58; Stamm, 127.

was only a part—was conducted by the Army in 1876 in the Powder River Basin, meanwhile, young Shoshone men from their reservation and young Arapaho men from the Red Cloud Agency realized that scouting for the generals offered both an honorable occupation and food for their families.

About 120 Shoshone warriors, led by Wisha, Nawkee and Luishaw, joined Gen. George Crook as scouts in his drive that ended at the Battle of the Rosebud, shortly before the Custer disaster. The Shoshone scouts received Army rations; while they were away, their families drew food rations from Army stores at Camp Brown.

For their part, Arapaho leaders still hoped that by cultivating friendships with officers they might yet find Army support for a reservation of their own.

As a result, both Shoshone and Arapaho scouts, together with 100 Pawnees and a few Lakota, were all with Gen. Crook during a campaign in November 1876 when his troops attacked a large Cheyenne camp under Dull Knife on the headwaters of Powder River. The Army pursued the remaining Oglala and Cheyenne bands through the winter. The following spring, all came in to the Lakota agencies. The wars of the northern plains were essentially over.[16]

The Northern Arapahos, however, still had no reservation.

THE NORTHERN ARAPAHO ARRIVAL ON WIND RIVER

According to the Arapahos, Gen. Crook in 1877 agreed to help them find a reservation on Tongue River, near the northern end of the Powder River Basin. Nothing would come of that, but other Army officers also pushed for a place for them north of the North Platte.

In September 1877, Arapaho leaders Friday, Black Coal, Sharpnose and 16 Lakotas, including Red Cloud and Spotted Tail,

16   Fowler, 58-63; Stamm, 113-114. 128.

traveled to Washington, D.C., to meet with President Rutherford B. Hayes and Interior Secretary Carl Schurz.

Black Coal made an eloquent plea for a home for the Northern Arapaho. "You ought to take pity on us and give us good land, so that we can remain upon it and call it our home," he said to the president, the secretary and a group of Army officers.[17]

Hayes approved a temporary location for the Arapaho that winter on the Sweetwater—on the route they would need to travel from the Red Cloud Agency to the Shoshone Indian Reservation. By this time, James Irwin, agent on the Shoshone Reservation at the time of the Brunot Cession, was now agent at the Red Cloud Agency. The Indian Bureau sent him to talk with Washakie. According to farmer Fin Burnett, Shoshone leaders Washakie, Norkok, Wahwannabiddie, Moonhabe and Wesaw agreed to make peace with the Arapahos and to allow them a place—just temporarily—on their reservation.[18]

At Red Cloud Agency in Nebraska in the fall of 1877, the 950 or so Northern Arapahos were issued 155 cattle to feed them on their journey. They left Oct. 31. They arrived at Fort Fetterman on the North Platte on Nov. 13; by Nov. 18, they had killed and eaten all the cattle. Gen. Crook approved an issue of guns and ammunition to the men so that they could hunt. They continued moving and spent the coldest months of the winter near the Sweetwater-North Platte confluence, in the country around Independence Rock.

On March 18, 1878, 21 Arapaho lodges under Black Coal's leadership arrived, with a military escort, on the Shoshone Reservation on Wind River and camped two days' travel from the agency headquarters at Camp Brown.

Reluctantly, Shoshone Reservation Agent James Patten issued rations for the Arapaho. Within a few weeks, leaders of

---

17   Fowler, 65.
18   Stamm, 129.

both tribes met informally. Patten reported the Shoshone continued to object, but were willing to accept the Arapaho, for now. Both tribes continued to hope for a meeting with Gen. Crook—and a better solution. By May, most of the remaining Arapaho arrived on Wind River.[19]

"Thus began," writes ethnohistorian Loretta Fowler about the Northern Arapaho, "a struggle to subsist on short rations, to counter the Shoshones' efforts to have them removed, and to resist the government's attempts to undermine tribal institutions."[20] As for the Eastern Shoshones, they too faced a short food supply and government pressure against their traditions—and they were now forced to share their reservation with these newcomers, their enemies in warfare only a few years earlier, whether they liked it or not.

THE LAWSUIT

In 1927, the Shoshone successfully petitioned the 69th U.S. Congress to pass a jurisdictional act, which then enabled the Shoshone Tribe to sue the U.S. Government for a violation of the Fort Bridger Treaty of 1868.[21] Before the 1946 Indian Claims Commission Act, tribes were required to have special jurisdictional acts passed, which allowed tribes to make a specific claim against the U.S. government.[22]

The Fort Bridger Treaty established the reservation in the Wind River valley for the "absolute and undisturbed use and occupation of the Shoshonee Indians."[23] By 1927, the Arapaho had

---

19   Fowler, 63-67; Stamm, 128-129; John Washakie, email to WyoHitory.org Editor Tom Rea, June 13, 2018.
20   Fowler, 67.
21   *Statutes at Large*. 69th Congress, 2nd Session. Public Law 69-705 (S. 5523). Chapter 302. Thursday, March 3, 1927,1349-1350.
22   Anna Price, "American Indian Law: A Beginner's Guide, US Federal Law, Court Cases", (Law Library of Congress, 2022).
23   Article 2, Fort Bridger Treaty of 1868, Dated July 3, 1868, Ratified Feb. 26, 1869, and Proclaimed Feb. 24, 1869. Compiled and edited by Charles J. Kappler. (Washington: Government Printing Office, 1904).

been on the reservation for nearly 50 years and during that time, the Commissioner of Indian Affairs held "that the Arapahoes have equal rights to the land on the said reservation which does not depend upon the further consent of the Shoshones..." The Shoshone rejected the notion that they had willingly given up half the reservation to the Arapaho. In their suit against the U.S., they claimed that "the guardianship of the United States over the property and affairs of tribal Indians does not enable the Government to require a tribe to which an exclusive right of occupancy has been pledged by treaty to share it with another tribe without just compensation." [24]

THE RULING

In 1937, the U.S. Supreme Court ruled in favor of the Shoshone, stating that the U.S.government had indeed unlawfully appropriated the land. The U.S. government was ordered to pay the Shoshone tribe over $4 million in compensation for the shared interest in the land. This ruling compensated the Shoshone for the loss of their "undivided interest" in the land and legally established that the reservation was now a joint territory belonging to both tribes.

Following the Supreme Court ruling, Congress approved details of the settlement in a separate law passed July 27, 1939, which specifically dealt with the distribution of the judgment fund to the Shoshone. This act further cemented the shared status of the reservation by referencing the two tribes as co-owners and by establishing a framework for their joint management of the reservation. The name of the reservation was officially changed to the Wind River Indian Reservation to reflect the shared residency.

---

24   *Shoshone Tribe of Indians v. United States*, 299 U.S. 476 (1937).

Note: This chapter is adapted from a WyoHistory.org article funded by Wyoming Humanities as part of their project, "Two Nations, One Reservation" published Saturday, June 23, 2018.

https://www.wyohistory.org/encyclopedia/arapaho-arrive-two-nations-one-reservation

For Further Reading:

WyoHistory.org, *Two Nations, One Reservation,* Social Studies Lesson Plan, https://www.wyohistory.org/education/toolkit/two-nations-one-reservation

WIND RIVER INDIAN RESERVATION: EARLY YEARS & CONTEXT

Stamm IV, Henry E. *People of the Wind River: The Eastern Shoshones, 1825-1900.* University of Oklahoma Press, 1999. Core monograph on treaty making, leadership, economy, and early agency years.

Markley, Elinor, and Beatrice Crofts (eds.). *Walk Softly, This Is God's Country: Sixty-Six Years on the Wind River Indian Reservation: The Letters and Journals of the Rev. John Roberts, 1883-1949.* Mortimore Publishing, 1997. Missionary letters giving detailed, on-the-ground accounts from the reservation's first generations.

O'Gara, Geoffrey. *What You See in Clear Water: Life on the Wind River Reservation.* New York: Knopf, 2000. Narrative centered on water rights; helpful for long-view institutional history rooted in 19th-century treaties.

Hebard, Grace Raymond. *Washakie: Chief of the Shoshones.* Originally 1930; University of Nebraska Press reprint, 1996. Foundational (if dated) account of Shoshone leadership during the reservation's formation.

Fowler, Loretta. *Arapahoe Politics, 1851-1978: Symbols in Crises of Authority.* University of Nebraska Press, 1982. Indispensable context on the Northern Arapaho after 1878 co-location at Wind River.

Chapter 3

A NEW WAY OF LIFE:
THE INFLUENCE OF THE WHITE MAN

The coming of settlers and the beginning of political and economic encounters with non-Indians forced many Indian nations to develop government systems which were compatible with dealing with colonists, frontiersmen, traders, and army personnel. Some tribes, like the Cherokee, developed constitutions and organized government in much the same way as the U.S. government, with three branches performing legislative, judicial, and executive functions.

However, many tribes kept traditional tribal consensus governments in place long after the last treaty was enacted in 1871. The Shoshones and Arapahos went through a gradual evolution from completely traditional tribal consensus governments to the form government practiced today, with its general councils, business councils, and the Wind River Inter-Tribal Council—today's Joint Business Council — made up of members from both tribes. The influence of agents assigned to the reservations, as well as the allotment program, which broke up traditional family units, hurried the erosion of

KEY NAMES AND TERMS
• Dawes Act
• Reserved rights doctrine
• Treaty
• Snyder Act
• Indian Self Determination and Education Assistance Act of 1975
• Bureaucracy
• Allotment
• Removal
• 1st Treaty of Ft. Bridger
• Shoshone Agency
• Brunot Cession
• Riverton Reclamation Project
• BIA

traditional ways among these tribes and escalated the adoption of non-Indian ways of governing.

Nevertheless, the Wind River tribes clung to some of their more valued beliefs about the role of government among their peoples. Modern government on the Wind River Reservation represents a blend of traditional native ways and governing patterns of the larger culture.

THE GENERAL ALLOTMENT ACT OF 1887

One of the major influences on early reservation life which continues today was the General Allotment Act of 1887. Also known as the Dawes Act for its sponsor, Senator Henry Dawes of Massachusetts, the act broke up the communal ownership of land by tribes and allowed for allotments to individual tribal members. After 25 years, individuals were to be issued "fee" or individually-owned title to the land to sell or keep as they chose. Additionally, the law allowed the government to open for purchase and settlement by non-Indians those lands not used for individual tribal allotments.[1]

Some of those in favor of this legislation had a desire to replace tribal culture with the culture of Anglo-Americans. The breaking up of tribal groups through allotment was one way of facilitating assimilation into the larger culture and increasing acculturation overall, proponents argued. Some supporters of the bill who were genuine friends of the Indian tribes thought individual ownership of tribal lands would protect them from further encroachment by avaricious individuals and corporations, such as railroad companies.

By authorization of the president of the United States, reservation land could be allotted according to a formula which gave one quarter section (160 acres) to each head of a family, and lesser

---

1   W. E. Washburn, *The Assault on Indian Tribalism: The General Allotment Law (Dawes Act of 1887).* (Philadelphia: J. B. Lippincott Co., 1975), 68-74.

amounts to single Indians and children.[2]

In 1891, an amendment to the Dawes Act gave the Secretary of the Interior the power to lease allotted land to whomever he wished if the Indian who owned the allotment did not use it in the way he was expected to. Any Indian who did not "personally and with benefit to himself occupy or improve his allotment or any part thereof" could lose his allotment.[3]

CONSEQUENCES OF THE DAWES ACT
The General Allotment Act of 1887

Determined in part the amount of Indian land available to non-Indians

Determined some citizenship rights for Indians

Altered tribal authority toward more emphasis on individual authority (vs. communal authority)

Divided communal Indian lands into individual parcels

Changed previous treaty commitments

Empowering the Secretary of the Interior to determine if land was being used as "expected" left much room for interpretation and abuse, with no thought to future use or needs by the individual tribal member's descendants or the tribe as a whole. The idea of allotment was not new. Many treaties prior to the Dawes Act contained provisions for allotment of land to individual Indians. Usually, however, allotments under treaty provisions did not provide for free and clear titles to Indians, a fact, which, ironically, led some Indian supporters to work for passage of the Dawes Act, even though the idea of individual ownership was completely counter to Indian tribal cultural values and work ethics.[4]

These supporters, including several prominent Eastern

2   *U. S. Statutes at Large,* Vol. 24, 388-391.
3   Deloria, 10.
4   Washburn, 11.

liberals and religious leaders, felt that if the Indians were given individual titles to their lands, they would be safe from the non-Indian encroachment which took place all during the 1800s. They had watched the tragedy of the removal program, where whole tribes were moved, against their will, out of ancestral homelands and into often unfamiliar places[5]. The result was illness and death for many. The Dawes Act seemed like a way to prevent such tragedy, and to protect lands granted under treaty to various tribes.

Other humanitarian supporters of the tribes believed that a philosophy of individualism and the hard work required of farming life were in the tribe's best interests and would contribute to their assimilation into American life, which they saw as both necessary and healthy. If one remembers the times, and the fact that other ethnic groups certainly weren't granted the same rights and privileges of white Americans (i.e., slavery for African Americans had just been outlawed), these attitudes can be viewed as extremely sympathetic to the Indian cause.

Nevertheless, not everyone was in favor of the passage of the Dawes Act, and vigorous debate on the merits of the bill was held. Some members of the House Committee on Indian Affairs had serious doubts about the wisdom of this bill, arguing in the minority report of the committee that:

However much we may differ with the humanitarians who are riding this hobby, we are certain that they will agree with us in the proposition that it does not make a farmer out of an Indian to give him a quarter section of land. There are hundreds of thousands of white men, rich with the experiences of centuries of Anglo-Saxon

---

5   Theda Perdue, Michael D. Green, Colin Calloway (ed). *The Cherokee Nation and the Trail of Tears: The Penguin Library of American Indian History Series* (Viking Press, 2007); Joseph Bruchac, *Navajo Long Walk: Tragic Story of a Proud Peoples Forced March from Homeland* (National Geographic Kids, 2002).

civilization, who cannot be transformed into cultivators of the land by any such gift.[6]

They also charged that:

The real aim of this bill is to get at the Indian lands and open them up to settlement. The provisions for the apparent benefit of the Indian are but the pretext to get at his lands and occupy them... If this were done in the name of Greed, it would be bad enough; but to do it in the name of Humanity, and under the cloak of an ardent desire to promote the Indian's welfare by making him like ourselves, whether he will or not, is infinitely worse.[7]

History seems to have validated the claims of the minority report of the committee, as passage of the Act neither made farmers of Indians nor preserved their treaty lands. In fact, tribal lands were reduced from 138 million acres in 1887 to 48 million in 1934. Much of these remaining acres were poor farmland, an ironic fact in light of one of the original purposes of the allotment.

It was particularly difficult for Plains and Great Basin area tribes like the Eastern Shoshone and Northern Arapaho to attempt a sedentary agricultural life. Their nomadic lifestyle didn't include individual ownership of real estate or specific territorial boundaries. They were hunters and gatherers. Where there was food, there was home. Their culture was fashioned around following the buffalo and other game and gathering food where it could be found. This was in sharp contrast to other tribes like the Iroquois, who had a sedentary agricultural lifestyle which included family ownership of property.

The General Allotment Act did much more than simply

---

6   House Report No. 1576, 46 Congress, 2 session, serial 1938, cited in Otis, D. S., *The Dawes Act and the Allotment of Indian Lands* (University of Oklahoma Press), 12.

7   House Report No. 1576, p. 19.

divide tribal lands among individual Indians. It also played a role in determining how much land the tribes would keep and how much would be open to acquisition by others, what citizenship rights Indians would have (because the bill tied land ownership to citizenship), what authority would be vested in the tribe or the individual, whether treaties would be honored or broken, and other similar and far-reaching issues.[8] Not all of these questions were explicitly stated in the Dawes Act. Because they were implicit in the terms of the act, however, the Dawes Act has had more impact upon the history of the tribes and Indian culture than almost any other single piece of legislation; and this impact continues today.

For the tribes at Wind River, allotment raised a legal issue without precedent—the inheritance of real property. The family structure of the Shoshone and Arapaho tribes, as well as the business of tribal government, were irrevocably altered as American inheritance laws were adopted. Individual family members and tribal councils became concerned with previously nonexistent issues of land ownership. It is doubtful that all the bill's supporters realized the sweeping impact of what they were enacting until many years later, if ever.

The General Allotment Act continues to play a significant role in the lives of the Tribal members of the Wind River Reservation. For many years, because Tribal members could not hold clear title to their land, as it was held in "trust" by the Department of the Interior, this trust land could not be mortgaged or used as collateral for a home (or any kind of) loan. This simple fact made the home and farm/ranch ownership that many Americans enjoy out of the reach of most Tribal members who held "trust" land. Beginning in the early 2000s, the Bureau of Indian Affairs began to approve mortgages on trust and restricted

---

8   Washburn, 3.

land in Indian Country, including Leasehold Mortgages and Trust Land Mortgages.[9] While well intended, the ruling that allows these mortgages, the "Section 184 Indian Home Loan Guarantee Program," has considerable complexities that are difficult to navigate and while it is a valuable tool for increasing Native American homeownership overall, its effectiveness is impacted by factors related to the specific tribal communities and the availability of participating lenders.[10]

THE BUREAU OF INDIAN AFFAIRS

In colonial days, Indians far outnumbered early colonists. They also had great military prowess, well-organized governments, and the advantages of knowing their lands and resources far better than the new European colonists. Because of this, the first presidents, their cabinets, and Congress paid serious attention to Indians. The Continental Congress had three different departments to deal with Indian affairs on a nation-to-nation basis in three geographical regions.[11]

Government trading houses for Indians were set up at the end of the 18th century and a superintendent of such trade was appointed in 1806. In 1817, federal statute authorized the use of U. S. courts for Indians and non-Indians who broke the law. For the first time, teachers, agricultural specialists, and others were sent by the government to "civilize and Americanize" the Indian population in the United States.[12]

Governors of the territories of the U.S. were also closely involved in Indian affairs. Though they reported to the Secretary

---

9   "Mortgages in Indian Country," *U.S. Department of the Interior, Bureau of Indian Affairs.* https://www.bia.gov/service/mortgages
10   "Pros & Cons of Section 184 Loans for Native Home Ownership," *Partnership with Native Americans.* https://nativepartnership.org/blog/history-culture-justice-category/pros-cons-of-section-184-loans-for-native-home-ownership
11   T.W. Taylor, *The Bureau of Indian Affairs* (Boulder, CO: Westview Press, 1984), 33.
12   Ibid.

of State in relation to territorial issues, they reported to the Secretary of War in connection with Indian issues.[13] Many of these men were instrumental in negotiating Indian treaties and in securing title to Indian lands.

In 1824, Secretary of War John C. Calhoun created the Bureau of Indian Affairs (BIA) under the War Department and assigned it the duties of approval of government expenditures in relation to Indian affairs, appropriation of annuity funds (funds paid to tribes under treaty terms, as compensation for lands ceded), settlement of Indian/non-Indian trade claims, oversight of government monies spent to "civilize" the tribes, and all other general correspondence related to Indians.[14] In 1832, Congress formalized the existence of the BIA within the War Department. In 1849, the BIA was transferred to the Department of Interior.

From its beginning in 1824 with one national head and two clerks as staff, the BIA mushroomed to more than 16,000 employees by the 1980s.[15] In addition to agents on the reservations, farmers, doctors, blacksmiths, carpenters and others were employed by the BIA. A large proportion of BIA employees in the 1800s and early 1900s were teachers.

The breakup of communal land holdings by the tribes through allotment, the restriction of Indians to their reservations, which resulted in the need to provide rations and other subsistence aid, and the granting of citizenship to Indians resulted in the transfer of much government on reservations from the tribes to BIA agents and staff.

One of the effects of the General Allotment Act of 1887 was the involvement of the BIA in recording and monitoring tribal enrollment and assessment of tribal land values. From 1888 to 1911, the number of BIA employees tripled, largely to deal

---

13   Taylor, 34.
14   Ibid.
15   Taylor, 35.

with all the administrative duties related to allotment, including surveys, sale of land, enforcement of land dealings, etc.

The Snyder Act of 1921 gave formal authority to the vast role of the BIA in Indian Affairs, which by then included custody of Indian money, both tribal and individual, approval of wills and determination of heirs, policing of reservations and punishment of offenders, aiding religious missions, promoting economic devel-opment, especially agricultural endeavors such as construction of irrigation and supervision of livestock operations, and discouraging liquor on reservations.[16]

DEVELOPMENT OF THE BUREAU OF INDIAN AFFAIRS

1806 Government trading houses established

1817 U.S. courts authorized by statute to deal with violations of the law on reservations

1819 President authorized to hire teachers, agricultural specialists and other skilled craftsmen to instruct Indians on reservations

1824 BIA created within the War Department

1832 BIA given statutory authority by Congress

1849 BIA transferred to Department of the Interior

As a result of a national movement for reform and reorganization among Indian tribes from 1920-1940, and especially, as a result of the Great Depression, Congress passed the Indian Reorganization Act of 1934 (IRA) or Indian New Deal. The IRA brought about many changes, including ending allotment of tribal lands and offering incentives for tribes to adopt constitutions and governing councils similar to the structure of the U.S. government.

In addition, by the 1940s, the BIA had become a huge, centralized bureaucracy which had become unwieldy to manage. In the years following World War II, the BIA underwent a move

---

16   Taylor, 20-38.

to decentralize the agency, with the creation of regional and area offices throughout the country. That basic structure is still in place today, though the functions have changed dramatically over time in some regions of the country. As a result, many previous BIA functions began to be transferred back to the tribes, to state governments, or even to county and local municipalities. In 1956, the Wind River Reservation Tribes assumed the responsibility for many functions previously managed by the BIA.

Not only did the Tribes take control of many governmental functions. Because the Indian Reorganization Act of 1934 decreed that Indians be given preference in BIA employment, approximately 75 percent of BIA staffers by the 1980s were Native American. On the Wind River Reservation, the number of Indian employees in the BIA was more than 90 percent of all employees in 1991. So, both local tribal government and BIA oversight began to reflect the leadership of enrolled tribal members.

Enacted in 1975 to give tribes more autonomy and control over the programs and services that serve them, the Indian Self-Determination and Education Assistance Act (ISDEAA), or Public Law 93-638, allows federally recognized tribes to contract with the federal government to receive funding and administer programs.[17] Today at Wind River, the local BIA superintendent is charged with the administration of many separate departments. Administrations of law enforcement on the reservation and maintenance, distribution and management of per capita monies (direct cash distributions, often from gaming revenue, that are divided equally among tribal citizens), facilities and grounds management, soil conservation and range management, and irrigation projects are some of the main responsibilities of the Wind River BIA.

The Indian Self Determination and Education Assistance

---

17   "Self-Determination," *U.S. Department of the Interior, Bureau of Indian Affairs*. https://www.bia.gov/regional-offices/great-plains/self-determination

Act of 1975 further reduced the authority and influence of the BIA, encouraging a system of self-government by the tribes in which they could contract and oversee government programs to the tribes without the direct supervision of the BIA. These agreements are often called "638" contracts, in reference to the number of the federal statute.[18] Beginning in 1989, child protection services, the largest single "social service" on the Wind River Reservation, is provided by each Tribe under contracts with the State of Wyoming and is supplemented with "638" funding.

The primary function and emphasis of the BIA on the national level, then, has moved from one of direct supervision, service, and control of the tribes in the 1800s and early 1900s to one of a contracting or granting agency, with indirect operational oversight responsibilities today. Evidence of this shift can be observed in the increase in federal grants and contracts directly to tribes since the 1990s. However, the amount of influence the BIA exerts over the tribes today is at least in part dependent on the wishes and actions of the tribes' general and business councils, and has evolved over time.

In the case of the Shoshone and Arapaho tribes, programs are contracted when the respective Tribal Council and Inter-Tribal Council is willing and able to administer the program themselves. Part of the reluctance of the Tribes to assume responsibility for their own management is that without the long-standing structure of the BIA, formally recognized and officed in Washington, the Tribes have to advocate for budget, resources, and reforms of contracted services, oftentimes requiring travel to regional offices or Washington, D.C. Other things complicating the assumption of wide scale reservation management duties by the tribes are that many of the programs are currently underfunded and understaffed. The tribes inherit those problems and have to

---

18   *Public Law*, 93-638, (1975).

expend considerable tribal monies to correct them. The shift in the BIA's function from direct intervention in tribal affairs to a more oversight-focused role, aimed at promoting tribal self-determination through the Indian Self-Determination and Education Assistance Act (ISDEAA), has presented several challenges. According to reports from the Government Accountability Office (GAO) and other sources, these challenges include:

- Lack of performance measurement and criteria: BIA's oversight capabilities are hindered by insufficient metrics to assess program effectiveness and hold the agency accountable for outcomes. This makes it difficult to track progress and identify areas for improvement in service delivery and program implementation.

- Slow awarding of grants: Tribes and tribal organizations face delays and inefficiencies in the grants process, impacting their ability to access and utilize essential federal funding for programs and initiatives. The GAO notes that workload increases, particularly related to the Inflation Reduction Act of 2022 (IRA) funding, exacerbate this issue, as limited staff and competing priorities strain the agency's capacity to process awards in a timely manner.

- Poor management by tribes: While the intention of ISDEAA is to empower tribes to manage their own programs, some instances of inadequate tribal management and fiscal control have arisen, leading to concerns about accountability and the effective use of federal funds. However, it is important to acknowledge that inadequate federal funding also limits tribal options for administering programs effectively, according to the GAO.

- Questionable fiscal control by the BIA: Concerns regarding

BIA's financial oversight and its ability to properly manage and account for tribal trust funds and other financial resources persist. This includes inadequate controls, data limitations, and a lack of proper reconciliation procedures, impacting the accuracy and transparency of BIA's financial operations. In some cases, as noted by the GAO in their October 2023 report, data accuracy and completeness issues hinder the analysis of real estate services data, further highlighting challenges in BIA's financial and operational management.

These problems underscore the complexities inherent in shifting from direct management to an oversight role, particularly within a historically strained relationship between the federal government and tribal nations. Addressing these issues is crucial for ensuring the success of tribal self-determination and the effective delivery of services to American Indians and Alaska Natives.

ESTABLISHMENT OF THE RESERVATION

Within a decade of the arrival of the British colonists on the eastern shores of the United States, fighting between Indian tribes and the newly arrived settlers broke out. Idealistic notions of living together in harmony were quickly shattered as the vast differences between the colonial culture and that of the different tribes became apparent.

Over the course of the 1800s, many battles were fought between various tribes and non-Indian settlers, trappers and traders, and the army, expanding ever westward across the continent into the territories of the new and different tribes, eventually including the Plains and Great Basin areas of the Eastern Shoshone and the Northern Arapaho. Before the end of the century, the battles were dying out and Indians everywhere were entering into treaties with the government as both parties strove to end the bitter struggle between them and to protect their individual interests.

The first treaty negotiated by the fledgling United States with the Indians was in 1778. The last was in 1871, when an amendment to an appropriations bill before the Congress stated that Indian Nations would no longer be recognized for the purpose of treaty making. Treaty making went on for nearly 50 more years, until 1914, when the last major treaty between the U.S. government and Indians was ratified between the Ute Indians and the government. From 1871 forward, however, such treaties were referred to as agreements.

A treaty is a contract between sovereign nations and is considered the "supreme law of the land", superior to laws passed by states and equal to Congressional acts.[19] The act of entering into treaties with the Indians was an acknowledgment of Indian sovereignty, of their status as independent nations, not under the control of or subject to the laws of the United States. More than 600 treaties with Indian tribes have been entered into over the years.

The end of the formal treaty period in 1871 also marked the end of the federal government's recognition of the sovereignty of Indian nations. From then on, all Indian matters were dealt with through legislation, which did not require the participation and agreement of Indian leaders. The status of Indian sovereignty is still a controversial issue among Indians and non-Indians today, in spite of this federal action. (For more on the concept of sovereignty, see Chapter 5).

Treaties are considered by Supreme Court rulings to be grants of rights from Indians, not grants of rights to them. Therefore, any right which is not expressly outlawed by federal statute or treaty is reserved to the tribes. This is known as the

---

19   S.L. Pevar, *The Rights of Indians and Tribes*, ACLU Handbook, (New York/ Toronto: Bantam Books, 1983), 32.

"reserved rights" doctrine.[20]

Treaties between the U. S. and the tribes were initially voluntary, because the Indians possessed power equal to or in some cases superior to the colonists in the early days. The colonists wanted Indian land and protection, and the tribes wanted goods and services the colonies had to offer. After the War of 1812, when British power over the U. S. was ended, things began to change. Thousands of prospectors, settlers, and government military men moved westward, gradually decimating the Indian tribes. Smallpox and other deadly diseases also moved west, decimating native populations by up to 90%. Many of the treaties that followed were hardly voluntary, as the tribes were no longer in a position to bargain equally. However, such claims must be made cautiously, as it is impossible in many cases to impute will after the fact; that is, to know to what degree Indians entered into them voluntarily or by coercion.

The chief result of these treaties was the enclosure of tribes within reservations, sometimes far from their homelands.

Two general conditions of most treaties were 1) the relinquishment of tribal land to the U. S. government, and 2) the creation of reservations where tribal members could live under federal protection. Services to be provided by the government were included in some treaties and not in others.

One of the problems in this treaty-making process was that some of the treaties and agreements were negotiated by the government with the wrong people—Indians not empowered to make such decisions. This lack of clear understanding of tribal leadership on the part of government officials led to frequent misunderstandings and more than one war, as Indians reacted to treaty provisions as though they were null and void.

Another common problem was that Indians didn't always

---

20   Ibid.

know exactly what was in the treaties before signing them. They were written in English which few tribal leaders could read, and changes were sometimes made after negotiations had been concluded, especially toward the end of the treaty-making period when it is now clear that the U.S. government frequently took advantage of the tribes with whom they negotiated.[21] It was at best an uncertain and politically uneven process.

Some authorities view the treaty making process with the tribes as generally fair, holding that Indians got terms which satisfied them and were seen as just.[22] However, many successful monetary claims against the government for unfair dealings in various treaties have subsequently been awarded to tribes around the nation under the provisions of the Indian Claims Commission, a commission created by Congress in 1946 to address American Indians' claims against the government in a more just and expeditious manner. The act was intended to show gratitude to American Indians for their service in World War II.[23]

Whether these awards constitute clear evidence of unfair treatment of tribes by the U.S. government in specific cases is difficult to judge. This commission doubtless reflected the biases, values, and political climate of its time. The distressing and ongoing consequences of much of U.S. policy toward Native Americans in the nation's formative years are clear; whether individual treaties were mutually understood and favored by both government and tribal leaders at the time of ratification is less clear so many years after the fact.

WIND RIVER TREATIES

The Wind River Reservation was formally established under the treaty of 1868, generally called the Second Treaty of Fort Bridger,

---

21   Deloria, 5.
22   Cohen, 40-6.
23   Deloria, 6.

between the federal government and the eastern band of the Shoshone tribe. The reservation was to be known as the Shoshone Reservation. In this same treaty, the government also negotiated with the Bannock Indians for the establishment of their reservation in Idaho. Chief Washakie, seven other Shoshones, and six Bannock Indians approved the treaty by signing an "X" mark after their names, and several U.S. Army and other government representatives signed it also.[24] It is important to note that, at this time, the Arapaho were not involved at all, coming to the Shoshone Reservation only later, under pressure from the U.S. government and against the wishes of Shoshone leaders.

The First Treaty of Fort Bridger of 1863, executed five years earlier between the Shoshone government and the U.S. government, outlined generally the borders of Shoshone territory, established peaceful relations between the tribe and the U.S. government, provided for safe travel through and settlement by the U.S. military and other non Indian travelers in Shoshone country, and set compensation to the tribe for game lost as a result of such traffic.

In this treaty, provisions were made for construction of telegraph and railroad lines through Shoshone country. Stage lines and other non-Shoshone travelers were to be allowed to cross through as needed. Compensation for loss of game was arranged in the amount of $200,000 over a period of twenty years, and some clothing and provisions were provided at the time of the treaty. The $200,000 was not to be paid in cash, but in "articles the President of the United States may deem suitable to their wants."[25] The territory described as Shoshone country by this 1863 treaty was vast, including parts of Colorado, Utah, Idaho and Wyoming, and stretching over an area of approximately 45

---

24   Charles J. Kappler, ed., *Indian Treaties 1778-1883* (New York: Interland Publishing Inc., 1973), 848-50, 1020-24.
25   Kappler, 849.

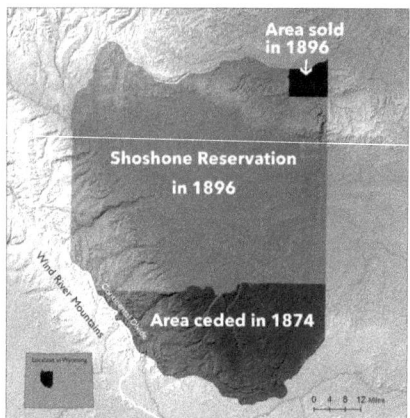

Shoshone Reservation, 1897, showing the hot springs sale, Wyoming Geographic Information Science Center, University of Wyoming.

million acres. (See map, p. 38)

The Second Treaty of Fort Bridger of 1868 fixed more definite and considerably smaller boundaries to the reservation, enclosing it entirely within an area of what is now central Wyoming. (See map, p. 42) The treaty expressed conditions for allotment of reservation lands to heads of families and individuals over 18 for the purpose of farming.[26]

In addition, the second treaty provided for the establishment of a BIA agent on the reservation and for schools for Indian children. Farm implements, seed, and financial incentives for Indians who were farming were to be doled out each year for several years in the form of goods purchased by the Secretary of the Interior. Clothing and material were to be provided for 30 years for all Indians on the reservation. Finally, the government was to furnish the reservation with a teacher, a doctor, a carpenter, and other skilled tradespeople to assist the Indians in converting to a new lifestyle.

In return, the Tribe was to stay within the confines of the reservation and uphold all the earlier 1863 treaty agreements concerning non-Indian passage through and construction on the Shoshone Reservation, diminished from 45 million acres to just 3 million.

This was the last official treaty with the Shoshone tribes, but not the last deal made with them. In 1867, gold was discovered

26   Kappler, 1020-24.

at South Pass near the southern edge of the reservation that would be established in 1868. Miners and some families poured in. The influx led to forced negotiations for the southern portion of the Shoshone Reservation, south of the Popo Agie River. By this time, Congress, as we have seen, had abandoned treaties in dealing with tribes

In exchange for $20,000 worth of cattle and $5,000 cash to be paid to Washakie over a five-year period, the tribe agreed to cede this part of the reservation to the government.[27] This land cession agreement, finalized in December of 1874, was called the Brunot Cession, after U.S. Commissioner Felix Brunot, who was involved in the deal. The ceded portion included the gold fields near South Pass, removing the Shoshone Tribe from realizing any royalties on the gold, and later iron ore, that was mined in the area.

In 1897, about 10 square miles of hot springs near what is now Thermopolis, Wyoming, were ceded to the U.S. government by Chief Washakie on behalf of the Shoshone Tribe. Washakie was able to negotiate the deal from an initial $50,000 offered by the U.S. government to $60,000. By this time, the Arapaho were living on the Shoshone Reservation, so Chief Sharpnose was invited to participate in the cession agreement by the government, even though the Arapaho tribe had no legal claim to the land in question. While the terms "exchange" and "agreement" imply a negotiation with two parties of equal standing, that is not how these negotiations unfolded. Washakie was faced with an impossible choice of agreeing to unfair terms or having the land taken forcibly without any compensation.

In April 1904, James McLaughlin, the government negotiator who had negotiated the hot springs sale, returned to Wind River with the new government proposal. He urged the tribes,

---

27   Ibid.

meeting jointly, to cede nearly 1.5 million acres of land, that is, about 2,300 square miles, north of Big Wind River. This would still leave the tribes more than 800,000 acres south of the river, and should, the government officials said, bring them revenues of more than $2.2 million. The tribes were to receive a minimum of $150,000 for an irrigation system, $50,000 in livestock, $50,000 for a school fund, and $50 for each Indian person. Any additional funds, after survey and map expenses, were to be used for the general benefit of the reservation tribes. In the long run, the tribes may only have gotten as much as $500,000.

This final cession of reservation land was signed on April 4, 1904. McLaughlin obtained signatures on the agreement from 202 of 247 eligible Shoshone men but only 80 of 237 Arapaho men—a majority of all the men on the reservation. But this was only a small minority of the Arapahos. The agreement ratified by Congress on March 3, 1905, had several amendments, not agreed to by the tribes. Arapaho head council chief Lone Bear sent a message to Washington on March 6: "We think treaty ratified by Congress not agree with original treaty signed by tribe." [28]

Ceded lands, in accordance with the agreement, were thrown open for homesteading the year after the tribes signed the document. On the edges of the Shoshone Reservation, the towns of Shoshoni, Riverton and Hudson had been founded in 1905 and 1906. Homesteaders were attracted by low prices of $1.50 per acre. An irrigation project of 300,000 acres was originally planned to benefit the homesteaders. The Wyoming Central Irrigation Company offered water to the farmers for a fee, with plans to use those fees to continue building the irrigation system. The farmers balked, wanting to wait to pay fees until water was actually available to them. Lawsuits followed. Most of the original

---

28   Loretta Fowler, *Arapaho Politics, 1851-1978: Symbols in Crises of Authority* (Lincoln, Neb.: University of Nebraska Press, 1982), 96.

homesteaders simply left.[29]

Under the 1905 congressional act, proceeds from land sales north of the river were to go to the tribes partly to finance irrigation on newly allotted lands south of the river. When the sales of the ceded lands produced much less than the projected revenue, the tribes did not receive the expected amount of payment for those lands, nor did they receive the promised cattle or the ditches and water rights they had been expecting.[30]

Even so, the Indian people were charged irrigation fees whether or not they used the new ditches, as government officials by this time were hoping to recoup from the Indians the losses the government faced as a result of the sluggish land sales. That is, instead of reimbursing the tribes for lands they'd already given up, the government charged the allottees for bringing water to their plots—before the water ever arrived. If the Indians could not pay the fees, officials pressed them to sell the land. White speculators, seeing possible opportunity in the situation, advertised for buyers in eastern cities. Many allottees sold their lands for a fraction of their worth.[31]

In the 1920s, when the U.S. Bureau of Reclamation worked on the development of the irrigation system, one serving the newly settled farmers exclusively, it became known as the Riverton Reclamation Project. There would be several more "withdrawals" of trust land by the bureau over the next few decades.

In 1939, the portions of this land not in fee patent status, that is, privately owned, by non-Native settlers and excepting the Riverton Reclamation project were restored to the tribes by federal statute, after pressure from the tribes and sympathetic politicians. This included land that was deemed unfarmable,

---

29   Fowler, 130.
30   Ibid.
31   Geoffrey O'Gara, *What You See in Clear Water* (New York: Knopf, 2000), 40-41; Fowler, 130-131.

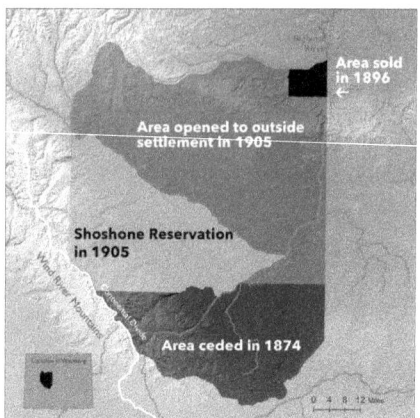

Shoshone Reservation, 1905, showing areas newly opened to outside settlement, Wyoming Geographic Information Science Center, University of Wyoming.

non-irrigated, and would not sustain ranching operations, or any other land not purchased by non-Native people. This restoration of ownership back to the Tribes via the BIA trust relationship accounts for the "checkerboard" mix of land ownership north of the Big Wind River. Interestingly enough, the Tribes always retained the subsurface mineral rights to these settlement lands. Some of the largest oil and gas producing fields are located in this area of the reservation.

The Arapaho were not residents of the Shoshone Reservation at the time of its creation, as has been noted. It wasn't until 1878, ten years after the Second Treaty of Fort Bridger, that the Arapaho came to live on the Shoshone Reservation. The Arapahos, along with the Cheyenne, had been promised their own territory, extending from southern Wyoming through a large portion of northern Colorado and into the western corners of Kansas and Nebraska through an earlier treaty between the government and several Plains tribes, the Fort Laramie Treaty of 1851.

As explained in Chapter 2, the Arapaho were never able to establish a permanent reservation in that area as promised by the U.S. government. Over the next few decades, Arapaho leaders strongly resisted federal efforts to move them south to Oklahoma and away from their homeland, and eventually, the Arapaho came to Wind River, where they remain. Not quite 1,000 Arapaho were taken by military escort to the Shoshone Agency in the spring of 1878 for "temporary keeping." They were never moved, in spite

Arapaho Chief Yellow Calf signs the agreement ceding lands north of the Wind River, 1904. Congress, without consulting the tribes, later amended it. Government negotiator James McLaughlin is at the table in a dark coat. Dick Washakie, son of the recently deceased chief, is standing in the front row on the left, hat in hand, badge on his vest. University of Wyoming American Heritage Center.

of protests by the Shoshone Tribe.

In 1927, the Shoshone Tribe petitioned congress for a juris-dictional act, which would allow them to sue the United States for giving a portion of their lands to the Arapaho without permission or compensation. After ten years of litigation, in 1937, the tribe won a nearly $4.5 million settlement, and the Arapahos became permanent residents of the reservation, entitled to half its profits and area. No legal divisions were ever drawn up, but Arapaho tribe members live mainly in the areas surrounding Ethete, Arapahoe, and St. Stephen's Catholic Mission, while Shoshone tribe mem-bers live primarily at Fort Washakie, Crowheart, and Burris. The name Shoshone Reservation, sometimes called Shoshone Agency, was officially changed to Wind River Reservation following the settlement of the suit.

This is referred to as the "Tunison Settlement" or "Tunison" money, named after the tribe's attorney, George Tunison. Shoshone tribal members were "paid" for the half of reservation given to the Arapahos in the form of land trade, that is, land previously taken, livestock, and/or farm implements. The Arapaho tribe paid for their half of the reservation through the garnishment of its half of profits derived from oil and gas leases until the $4.5 million was paid off. The federal government never expended any of its own funds in the settlement, taking any costs associated with the lawsuit from future oil and gas royalties that they administer on behalf of each tribe. In the end, the Arapaho paid for what became their share of the reservation twice; first, by treaty concessions they made for a separate reservation in central Wyoming that was never granted by the U.S. government, and again by paying for their share of the Wind River Reservation through the relinquishment of oil and gas royalties.

SUMMARY

A full understanding of the enormity of the original Shoshone and Arapaho territories, compared with what the two tribes share today, is important in understanding the constraints of the current government of the Wind River Reservation. The reservation today is about 2.3 million acres, or approximately 3,800 square miles, a small fraction of the Shoshone territory as roughly described in the first 1863 Treaty with the Shoshone. Today, it is inhabited and jointly governed by the two tribes, with a combined total of nearly 10,000 members. The Arapahos, once merely guests on the reservation, outnumber Shoshones now, by a margin of two-to-one.

Much of the land, including the town of Riverton (population: approximately 10,000), has been sold to non-Indians as a result of allotment policies, so the actual acreage where Shoshone and Arapaho people reside in communities on the reservation is quite small by comparison to early territories. Still, at nearly 4,000 square miles, the Wind River Reservation is substantial, particularly in comparison with many other reservations around the country.

The change from a nomadic lifestyle, with its loosely defined and changing boundaries, to the establishment of the reservation way of life with a definite, bounded territory, complete with the BIA structure and management, was perhaps the single most profound influence on the evolution of modern tribal government at Wind River.

The passage of the General Allotment Act of 1887 was another major influence over the development of contemporary tribal government, not only at Wind River, but across the nation. This act permanently changed many tribes' long-standing practices regarding the use and ownership of land by shifting ownership to individuals, which in turn changed the scope of tribal authority and the role of tribal government. It even affected the citizenship status of Native Americans by tying rights of citizenship to land ownership.

For Further Reading:

FOUNDATIONAL OVERVIEWS
(TREATIES, LAW, POLICY)

Prucha, Francis Paul. *American Indian Treaties: The History of a Political Anomaly*. University of California Press, 1994. Authoritative synthesis of the treaty system's legal and political logic.

Prucha, Francis Paul. *The Great Father: The United States Government and the American Indians*. 2 vols. University of Nebraska Press, 1984; abridged ed. 1986. Classic narrative of federal Indian policy through the reservation era.

Washburn, Wilcomb E. *Red Man's Land/White Man's Law: The Past and Present Status of the American Indian*. 2nd ed., University of Oklahoma Press, 1995. Concise legal history from colonial doctrines through allotment and beyond.

Cohen, Felix S., et al., eds. *Cohen's Handbook of Federal Indian Law*. LexisNexis, multiple editions (orig. 1941/1942; latest editions ongoing). The standard legal treatise on federal Indian law.

Deloria, Vine Jr., and Raymond J. DeMallie, eds. *Documents of American Indian Diplomacy: Treaties, Agreements, and Conventions, 1775-1979*. University of Oklahoma Press, 1999. Indispensable documentary collection.

Kappler, Charles J., ed. *Indian Affairs: Laws and Treaties*. 7 vols., U.S. Government Printing Office, 1903-1941 (digitized). Principal compilation of treaties, statutes, and executive orders affecting tribes.

HOW LAW RESHAPED LAND & RESERVATIONS
(ALLOTMENT, DISCOVERY, SOVEREIGNTY)

Hoxie, Frederick E. *A Final Promise: The Campaign to Assimilate the Indians, 1880-1920*. University of Nebraska Press (Bison ed.), 2001. Core study of assimilation policy and its effects on reservation life.

Carlson, Leonard A. *Indians, Bureaucrats, and Land: The Dawes Act and the Decline of Indian Farming.* Greenwood Press, 1981. Economic analysis of allotment's consequences.

Banner, Stuart. *How the Indians Lost Their Land: Law and Power on the Frontier.* Belknap Press of Harvard University Press, 2005. Legal processes intertwined with coercion to transfer land in the West.

Robertson, Lindsay G. *Conquest by Law: How the Discovery of America Dispossessed Indigenous Peoples of Their Lands.* Oxford University Press, 2005. Focus on *Johnson v. M'Intosh* and the discovery doctrine.

Williams, Robert A., Jr. *The American Indian in Western Legal Thought: The Discourses of Conquest.* Oxford University Press, 1990. Intellectual history of conquest doctrines shaping Indian law.

Wilkinson, Charles F. *American Indians, Time, and the Law: Native Societies in a Modern Constitutional Democracy.* Yale University Press, 1987. Influential account of how Supreme Court eras shaped sovereignty and reservation powers.

Harring, Sidney L. *Crow Dog's Case: American Indian Sovereignty, Tribal Law, and United States Law in the Nineteenth Century.* Cambridge University Press, 1994. Pivotal case study of jurisdiction and the rise of federal control on reservations.

WESTERN & PLAINS (CONTEXT, ADMINISTRATION, AND RESOURCES)

Rockwell, Stephen J. *Indian Affairs and the Administrative State in the Nineteenth Century.* Cambridge University Press, 2010. How federal bureaucracy built reservation governance.

Blackhawk, Ned. *Violence over the Land: Indians and Empires in the Early American West.* Harvard University Press, 2006. Essential western context for legal-political shifts preceding reservation formation (esp. Great Basin/Plateau).

NORTHERN CHEYENNE
(TREATIES, REMOVAL, RESERVATION FORMATION)

Killsback, Leo K. *A Sovereign People: Indigenous Nationhood, Traditional Law, and the Covenants of the Cheyenne Nation.* Volume 2 of 2, Texas Tech University Press, 2019. Killsback, a citizen of the Northern Cheyenne Nation, reconstructs and rekindles an ancient Cheyenne world-ways of living and thinking that became casualties of colonization and forced assimilation. Spanning more than a millennium of antiquity and recovering stories and ideas interpreted from a Cheyenne worldview, the works' joint purpose is rooted as much in a decolonization roadmap as it is in preservation of culture and identity for the next generations of Cheyenne people. Dividing the story of the Cheyenne Nation into pre- and post-contact, A Sacred People and A Sovereign People lay out indigenously conceived possibilities for employing traditional worldviews to replace unhealthy and dysfunctional ones bred of territorial, cultural, and psychological colonization.

Powell, Peter J. *People of the Sacred Mountain: A History of the Northern Cheyenne Chiefs and Warrior Societies, 1830–1879.* 2 vols., Harper & Row/University of Oklahoma Press, 1981. Deep narrative with extensive treaty–war context; National Book Award winner.

Leiker, James N., and Ramon Powers. *The Northern Cheyenne Exodus in History and Memory.* University of Oklahoma Press, 2011. Interprets the 1878–79 exodus and its legal/political legacy for reservation creation.

Stands In Timber, John; ed. Margot Liberty. *Cheyenne Memories.* Yale University Press; later Bison edition. Oral histories spanning pre-treaty through early reservation years.

Sandoz, Mari. *Cheyenne Autumn.* University of Nebraska Press/Bison Books. Narrative of the exodus with policy context on forced removal and reservation policy.

EASTERN SHOSHONE &
EARLY WIND RIVER RESERVATION

Stamm IV, Henry E. *People of the Wind River: The Eastern Shoshones, 1825–1900.* University of Oklahoma Press, 1999. Core monograph on treaty-making, leadership (incl. Washakie), and early institutional life on the reservation.

Hebard, Grace Raymond. *Washakie: Chief of the Shoshones.* University of Nebraska Press, 1996 (reprint of 1930 edition). Foundational—read with modern critiques in mind—covering 1868 Fort Bridger treaty context and early reservation years.

Madsen, Brigham D. *The Shoshoni Frontier and the Bear River Massacre.* University of Utah Press, 1985. Key background to conflicts that set the stage for Shoshone treaty negotiations and reservation formation.

Madsen, Brigham D. *The Northern Shoshoni.* Caxton Printers, 1980. Ethnohistorical overview (Idaho/Utah/Wyoming) illuminating the broader Shoshone treaty/reservation story.

O'Gara, Geoffrey. *What You See in Clear Water: Life on the Wind River Reservation.* Alfred A. Knopf, 2000; Vintage reprint, 2002. Modern narrative centered on Wind River water rights linking back to 19th-century treaties.

Fowler, Loretta. *Arapahoe Politics, 1851–1978: Symbols in Crises of Authority.* University of Nebraska Press, 1982. Crucial context after the Northern Arapaho were placed with the Shoshone at Wind River in 1878.

Chapter 4

WIND RIVER: THE EARLY DAYS OF THE TRIBAL COUNCIL

Vine Deloria, Jr. and Clifford M. Lyte depict the evolution of Indian government in their book *American Indians, American Justice* in this way:

> *The experience of most of the western tribes can be best characterized as government-sponsored transformation of traditional forms into a more workable version of an informal council, which could be called upon by the agent whenever it became impossible for him to work without some form of approval from the people concerned. The Indian agent would gather together the most influential leaders of the bands or communities living on the reservation and ask them to form an ongoing council to assist him in whatever functions he felt could be delegated to them. Generally, this council reflected the original political subdivisions of the tribal past but also incorporated the democratic principles in which the agent believed, which usually meant one person/one vote in contrast to the traditional method of choosing leaders.*[1]

Gradually, over the course of the early 1900s, tribal councils replaced the chief/council system at Wind River and led to the formation of BIA-instituted business councils. Each tribe had a general council composed of all members of the tribe, and a business council of six members who dealt with individual

---

1   Deloria, 93.

political and business affairs. A Joint Business Council of the Shoshone and Arapaho tribes, made up of the six members of each tribe's council, was established in the mid-1930s and met regularly to deal with reservation business affecting both Tribes. A Court of Indian Offenses was created to handle some of the judicial functions of the tribes, though separation of power was by no means absolute in those days.

The body of the whole in each Tribe, the general council, was considered to be the sovereign political power within tribal government, though government agents sought to make the smaller representative councils, especially the Joint Business Council, more influential. This effort to de-emphasize the importance of input from the whole tribe was encouraged as part of the overall "detribalization" effort by the U.S. government, an effort to disengage Indians from their traditional forms of government and to adopt the representative democracy of the larger culture. In some cases, the erosion of Indian culture and government may have been well-intentioned or a result of simple ignorance of tribal values. It has been noted extensively by historians, however, that detribalization was a conscious effort on the part of federal officials to eradicate traditional Indian ways in order to gain control over the tribes and critical access to valuable resources and land owned by the tribes.

Council leaders from the Arapaho tribe often served until illness, old age, or death interrupted a man's term. Shoshone

---

KEY NAMES AND TERMS

- John Collier
- Detribalization
- General Council
- Business Council
- Joint Business Council
- Reuben Haas
- Consensus
- Wheeler-Howard Act
- Tribal autonomy
- Assimilation
- Representative democracy
- Per capita payments
- Termination
- Recall election
- Indian Reorganization Act

For a time, at least, a tipi served as a council house for the Arapaho near St. Michael's Mission at Ethete. Charles Sproul photo, Riverton Museum.

council leaders changed more frequently and were often younger, reflecting a difference in tribal attitudes toward leadership. Two of the well-respected and long-serving Arapaho council leaders during the 1900s were Lone Bear, for Lower Arapaho, and Yellow Calf, of the Ethete community.

Among the Shoshones, council members were sometimes people who had intermarried outside their tribe or children of intermarried couples. Council members with white relatives were often viewed as being more assertive in dealing with federal representatives and were sometimes relied upon by the Joint Business Council to make the case for both tribes.[2] Irene Meade, the first woman council member for either tribe, was such a council member. Meade was also a charter member of the Wyoming Mayflower Society through her father, Napoleon Bonaparte Kinnear.[3]

Though the Tribes interacted only marginally outside the council meetings and had many differences, they nevertheless embraced individual strengths of the representative tribe members in concluding council business. Whatever their differences, both Tribes recognized the wisdom in presenting a unified front

2   Fowler, 147.
3   Black and White Photographs, 78, *Virginia Cole Trenholm papers, 1929-1979*, American Heritage Center, University of Wyoming.

to the federal government, and so generally tried to work together in spite of stylistic or attitudinal differences and animosities.[4]

DETRIBALIZATION EFFORTS AT WIND RIVER

Government officials wanted to see the Tribes together as one body on the reservation, but historical and cultural differences between the two tribes, as well as their innate sense of tribal sovereignty, all but ensured challenges to forming a single consolidated government. However, while each Tribe maintained separate General Council meetings, they would generally not go against the other Tribe if consensus could not be reached. A compromise might be worked out, or, if opinion was sharply divided, both sides would table a controversial issue or fail to meet a quorum, rather than present disrespectful confrontations or a divided image. By the time a vote was taken on a particular issue, the count was nearly always unanimous across the council—in both Tribes. This process could be lengthy but reflected native values of political interaction.

The Arapaho and Shoshone Tribes resisted some assimilative procedures instituted by reservation agents and embraced others, as fit their needs. The Shoshone are generally thought to have favored "white" ways of governing more than the Arapaho, though this was not always the case. The transition from primarily judicial/mediational roles played by tribal leaders to the roles of today's council, which combines legislative and executive functions, was a slow and sometimes painful process for the Tribes.

Federal authorities of that period tried repeatedly to break up tribal authority systems by appointing young men from the Tribes to positions of authority, rather than more traditional and honored elders. In the 1920s and 1930s, Shoshone Agency Superintendent Rueben Haas was especially persistent in

---

4   Merle Haas, Arapaho tribe member and researcher, interview with the author, Wind River Reservation, 1991.

pressuring the Tribes to adopt non-Indian methods of government, pushing them to adopt a constitution and by-laws which undermined their traditional methods of government. He also encouraged and assisted Indian men in their 20s and 30s to seek election to business councils. Haas gave special help to younger tribe members who wanted to farm or raise livestock by offering revolving credit and organizing livestock cooperatives to create support in grazing and labor associated with ranching or farming enterprises.[5] At first, these programs seemed to prosper, attracting many young men from both Tribes. Eventually, however, partly because of inconsistent and unpredictable federal policies and poorly managed BIA implementation of the programs, many young Indians failed in their attempts to farm and ranch successfully.

This failure, unfortunately, led to ridicule by other Shoshones and Arapahos. Some of the elders charged that the young entrepreneurs were trying to behave like non-Indians, in ways that were not beneficial to the Tribes. BIA personnel felt that the influence of the elders in promoting such attitudes was a major barrier to making progress on the reservation.[6]

Nevertheless, Superintendent Hass' efforts to detribalize the Wind River Reservation peoples continued. For the first time in tribal history, members considered several drafts of a formal constitution for use in governing the Tribes, introduced by Haas.

The constitutions Haas proposed and lobbied for virtually eliminated decision-making through the general councils, replacing that with a method of governing modeled after the United States constitutional government. Under a constitutional system, a newly-formed Joint Business Council would wield more influence and control than the two Tribes' business councils and would make more decisions without formal input from the two

---

5   Fowler, 168-72.
6   Ibid.

Tribes' general councils than in the past.

The first proposed tribal constitution was drafted by Haas, with the help from representatives of the Tribes, in 1925. It minimized the role of the elders and set the minimum age for election to the council at 30, a much younger than customary age for councilmen. It also made council decisions binding, provided for an election by voice vote of councilmen, and empowered the council to sign leases on behalf of the Tribes.[7] Though Haas was able to secure at least the outward support of a portion of the tribal council members on this constitution, the document failed to win approval of the BIA, and so was rendered officially null and void. Also, some council members ignored the changes, continuing to conduct business as usual.

Haas tried two more times, in 1931 and again in 1934, to enact a constitution on the Wind River Reservation, each time including even more structure and control than in the previous document. Those later drafts provided for amending the constitution by vote of tribal council (further increasing the representative powers of the council through bypass of the general councils), for election by formal ballot, and for greater independence of the tribal council from the BIA. This last effort met with disapproval by Washington officials of the BIA. Though they wanted the Indians to assimilate into the larger culture and adopt non-Indian ways of governing, the officials asserted that the council was only an advisory body with no authority to transact business or call meetings.[8] Hence, all three constitutional drafts ultimately failed to win approval of either the BIA or the Tribes.

In spite of the failure of the early constitutional drafts themselves, some of the reforms outlined in them "stuck" and

---

7   Ibid.
8   Ibid. Today, the BIA recognizes the Business Council of each Tribe as its governing body and does not usually respond to motions passed by the general councils (the entire body of the tribe) unless and until the Business Council takes some action regarding that motion.

became regular practice on the reservation. For instance, by the mid-1930s, election of tribal council members by balloting was an accepted practice. But Haas' attempts to infuse the councils with young blood were only partially successful, with only about half of the council being made up of men under forty.

NATIONAL REFORM AND REORGANIZATION

While Superintendent Haas was at work at Wind River attempting to make the Tribes more "progressive," major efforts at tribal reform were underway in Washington. The person in charge of Indian affairs for the nation, Indian Commissioner John Collier, took significant strides from the outset of his term in 1933 to assist the tribes in political and economic reform.

Collier wanted to return power to the tribes on reservations throughout the United States so they could oversee their own internal affairs and function more independently from the BIA. Legislation proposed by Collier was one of the most important milestones in the history of tribal government. It called for the preservation of Indian lands and resources and their economic development for the benefit of the tribes, the establishment of a workable system of credit for Native Americans, vocational education for tribal members, and importantly, the right to incorporate and form businesses within the tribes. On June 18, 1934, the Indian Reorganization Act (IRA), also called the Wheeler-Howard Act, passed the Congress of the United States and was enacted into law.

Under this bill, land was no longer to be allotted to individual members of tribes. Instead, land would be kept in "trust" for the Indians by the federal government. All the tribes on reservations were given the right to choose by majority vote whether to accept the reorganization as outlined in the bill proposed by Collier. The tribes were given one year to accept or decline the provisions of the IRA.

Across the nation, a total of 258 elections were held in which 181 tribes voted to accept the provisions of the Wheeler-Howard Act. This represented about 130,000 Indians in America. Some 86,000 Indians from 77 tribes, including Wind River tribes, rejected the terms of the IRA.[9] Some tribes voted for adoption of other elements of the act, creating some confusion in ensuing years.

Though the majority of tribes in the United States voted to reorganize and incorporate, both Tribes on the Wind River Reservation felt they had more to gain from staying under the direction of the Bureau of Indian Affairs than in adopting a constitution and assuming a larger role in self government under this act.

At first glance, it might seem that the two Tribes would have jumped at the opportunity to exercise more self-government than had been possible in early reservation years. However, the vote of the combined Wind River Tribes and other tribes across the nation against the IRA was at least in part a reflection of tremendous distrust of the U.S. government.

Virtually all the previous treaties and agreements with the United States had been violated in some way, some more far-reaching than others, over the years. To the Shoshone and Arapaho Tribes, the provisions of this act, which would have put in trust with the government large sums of Indian monies, seemed like one more potentially empty promise. By this time (mid-1930s), the Indians had been disappointed by the government in relation to water rights and charges, administration of oil leases on Indian lands, and still unfulfilled treaty provisions.

Also, a major disadvantage of voting for IRA reorganization, with its provision for a constitution, was that all constitutions and tribal laws had to be approved by the Secretary of the Interior.

---

9   Deloria, 15.

Many tribes, including the Shoshone and Arapaho of Wind River, did not (and still do not) want this kind of "self-government"—one subject to federal approval of every constitutional detail.[10]

In 1934, several meetings were held with both the Shoshone and the Arapaho Tribes by Collier and representatives of the BIA, and General Councils were held in which all members of the Tribes had a chance to discuss the new proposal.

One of the greatest fears of the Wind River Tribes was that the consolidation of Indian lands and the reversal of the allotment policy would ultimately result in chaos and further demoralization on the reservation. They saw this program as one more loss of land to the U.S. government. They were nervous about changing the ownership and use of their lands, having experienced most changes to date as negative ones. The Tribes believed that without the individual allotment system, the elderly, the sick, and the children of the reservation would be neglected. With their strong support of communal values and protection of all tribal members equally, that fear operated intensely in their discussion.

In an unofficial vote on the measure, both the Shoshone and Arapaho Tribes, in separate General Council meetings, voted unanimously to reject the proposed reforms.[11]

The government did not give up, however, and continued to try to allay Indian fears throughout the year, meeting with them several times, in Washington and elsewhere. After these meetings, more tribal meetings were held, and once again, in an unofficial polling of tribal sentiment, the Tribes voted strongly against reorganization. Fewer than 10 Arapaho and Shoshone voted in favor of the bill's changes.[12]

---

10   John Washakie and Alfred Ward, Shoshone Councilmen, interview with the author, Wind River Reservation, July, 1991.
11   Fowler, 173-6.
12   Ibid.

During meetings between representatives of the Wind River Tribes and Collier, the government would not assure that Indians of the reservation would be exempted from paying fees for water use–which they saw as paying for what was rightfully theirs, anyway–or that changes in oil lease management on reservation land to ensure profit to the Tribes would be enacted. And none of the many past treaty violations were addressed.

PROVISIONS OF THE 1934 INDIAN REORGANIZATION ACT

Preservation of Indian lands and resources

Economic development by tribes

Constitutional government and the right to incorporate

Vocational education for tribe members

End of allotment of Indian lands

One of the most apparent issues was that the Tribes were still not receiving per capita payments from monies owed them by earlier deals with the federal government. Much tribal income was still being held in trust by the government, and what small amount was not held in trust was issued to individuals on the reservation primarily in small credit orders at local stores. If a Tribal member didn't need what stores had to sell, or if they didn't spend the whole amount on needed items, they simply did not receive a cash payment.

These factors combined to make the Tribes resist the reorganization. When discussions ended and the official vote was taken in June of 1935, reorganization was defeated, though a considerable turnaround had happened, especially among the Shoshones. The Shoshones passed the reform agenda by one slim vote, while the Arapaho voted against it by a margin of two-to-one.[13] Though the Shoshones had voted in favor of the bill, the BIA ruled that both Tribes had to accept its provisions before it

---

13   Ibid.

could be enacted.

In many ways, acceptance of the reform would have consolidated both Tribes into a single tribal government, and so the two sovereign nations rejected the proposal. To this day, the Shoshone and the Arapaho are under a system of government different from all other tribes in the nation, because they are two separate nations, neither with a constitution or laws that have to be approved by the Secretary of the Interior. Most tribes in the region are on reservations designated for a single tribe or band and are IRA tribes, having adopted the governmental structures outlined by the Act.

An advantage of governing without a constitution and by-laws is that there can be more flexibility in decisions, since everything is not "black or white". Also, tribal ordinances and council procedures are not subject to approval by the Secretary of Interior, like they would be under an IRA constitutional government. The Wind River tribes are free to adopt any of the constitutional provisions of IRA governments if they seem wise; the difference is that they are not subject to approval of the Secretary of Interior. This difference is seen as a key advantage by many tribe members.[14]

However, the Tribes' business councils are understood by tribal members to be empowered only to act on routine matters. Without guidelines for action in new situations and problems, as might exist within a constitution, the Business Councils are strictly limited in the scope of their authority and must bring any non-typical matters before the general councils. This tends to restrict the powers of the business councils and slows down the governmental process, but this constraint and conservatism is not necessarily seen as negative by the Tribes.

Though the Wind River tribes rejected the terms of

---

14   Washakie Interview.

Wheeler-Howard, political change nevertheless continued to occur on the reservation. The superintendent following Haas, Forrest Stone, also pressed hard for extensive revamping of tribal political processes during the late 1930s.

Stone forced a recall election of the 1935 business councils even though there were still two years left of council members' terms and worked diligently to reduce the influence of the elders in selecting council candidates, proposing procedural changes which circumvented the usual tribal process involving the elders. Finally, he introduced the idea of political districting on the reservation, the practice of voting only for candidates in one's residential area.

The 1930s marked the beginning of a major transition towards a more representative and more powerful form of government as the two tribes agreed to form a Joint Business Council as a pragmatic response to the unique situation of two tribes sharing a single reservation. The Joint Business Council was composed of representatives from each tribe's Tribal Business Council, who were accountable back to their respective tribes while representing their interests in joint decisions. This shared governance marked the beginning of a new era. Indeed, the '30s were a time of political unrest on the Wind River Reservation, as both the Shoshone and the Arapaho Tribes struggled to maintain important old ways while adapting to new political requirements and realities on the reservation.

The transition has been characterized by Loretta Fowler in her book, *Arapaho Politics: 1851–1978*, as a fight between the "old Indians" and the "schoolboys." Schoolboys was a term derogatorily applied by older tribe members to young, educated Indians who were eager to adopt non-Indian ways. The elder tribe members were not opposed to education of the young in general; they thought it was good to have educated Indians among them, and often encouraged their young to get schooling. It was the

The log Council House on the south fork of the Little Wind River near Fort Washakie, one of three community halls on the reservation, saw social gatherings and council meetings at least into the 1950s. Lander Pioneer Museum.

lack of loyalty to the elders and traditional tribal values which caused someone to be labeled a "schoolboy", and which caused deep political rifts within the Tribes. Certainly, the early boarding schools on the reservation were a prime source of this and many other disruptions to, and erosion of, tribal culture.[15] To some extent, these political factions exist on the reservation today.

Council members originally served four year terms of office. During this period, agency personnel succeeded in reducing the terms of business council members to two years. Some scholars of the Tribes believe this was a move to disrupt continuity and longevity on the council, making way for non-Indians to impose more "progressive" points of view.

Other efforts at detribalization by the BIA (known in those days as the Indian Office) included the prohibition of many ritual ceremonies and practices overseen by elders, such as the Sun Dance, the most important religious ceremony of the Tribes. The Sun Dance, which had been outlawed several times by the federal government, was successfully prohibited from being performed for 10 years, from 1913 to 1923, when Indians once again won official permission to reinstate it. Some ceremonial rituals were performed in secret, even though outlawed, helping preserve tribal rituals during these years.[16]

Part of the reason the Sun Dance was permitted again was

---

15   Haas Interview.
16   Ibid.

because it had been "Christianized" to pacify the non-Indian culture, eroding some of the original native symbolism and practices in the dance. The medicine pole in the center of the Sun Dance lodge, originally symbolizing Thunderbird, now stood for God, or the Creator. The twelve poles of Sun Dance Lodge, originally representing Thunderbird's twelve tail feathers, came to symbolize the apostles.[17]

Religious missionaries on the reservation were in a curious political position in relation to the evolution of government at Wind River. At times, they functioned in effect as agents of the U.S. government by encouraging the adoption of customs and values of the larger culture from which they came. At other times, they asserted their influence with federal officials on behalf of tribal chiefs, arguing for the preservation of native culture.[18]

Sometime in 1888 or 1889, the Ghost Dance, a religious ceremony prophesizing the end of white inhabitation of native lands and the return of those lands to Native Americans in a "new world", originated on the Walker River Reservation in western Nevada, with a Northern Paiute man named Wovoka or Jack Wilson as the visionary of the movement. It was believed that in addition to restoring original native lands to them, this new world would bring back to life their dead kin as well. Historian Justin Gage argues that the rapid spread of the Ghost Dance was facilitated by pre-existing intertribal networks. By early spring 1890, the Ghost Dance arrived on the Wind River Reservation. This dance was prohibited by federal agents for posing a threat to white rule. Because no such new world appeared as prophesized, Shoshone Indians abandoned the practice after a relatively short period and the Arapaho later followed suit.[19]

---

17   Trenholm, 40.
18   Haas Interview.
19   Justin Gage. *We Do Not Want the Gates Closed between Us: Native Networks and the Spread of the Ghost Dance* (Norman: Oklahoma University Press, 2020) and companion website, https://nativeamericannetworks.com/

CULTURAL AND POLITICAL INDEPENDENCE AT WIND RIVER

In spite of seeming acquiescence to non-Indian ways and federal policies, the two Tribes continued to exercise their own ways of government and to express their own values related to political life, especially in the connection of their spiritual lives to their daily decisions.

The religious authorities in 19th century Arapaho life, for example, were ceremonial elders who had attained the highest possible status and prestige within the Arapaho religion. These religious men sanctioned many tribal activities and decisions and were responsible for tribal ritual objects, such as the Sacred Pipe of the Arapaho. Though the Shoshone had similar ceremonial elders, tribal members contend that religion and politics are more separate than in Arapaho life, both then and now.[20] These religious leaders provided a unifying socio-political structure among the bands in pre-reservation days, and continue to exert influence over the business council form of government established on the reservations.

Government by consensus, within an overarching socialistic model, in which all goods and income were distributed fairly, was an important political consideration, especially within the Arapaho Tribe. Shoshone tribal members were comfortable with majority rule, though the wishes of the whole Tribe, as mandated through General Council meetings, were respected.[21] Combined with the native belief that good government flows partly from good relations with the Creator, a form of government emerged which, though outwardly resembling a representative democracy, actually reflected Native American values and priorities.

For instance, when BIA superintendents pressed the Tribes

---

20   Shoshone councilmen, interview with the author, Wind River Reservation, Fort Washakie, Wyoming, July 1991.
21   Washakie and Ward Interview.

to elect their councilmen by majority vote, the Arapahos quietly let their elders select the councilmen and then informed BIA officials of the "election" results. They commemorated these selections through the religious Eagle Drum Ceremony, conducted by Arapaho elders. The newly selected councilmen were publicly honored in a ceremony which reminded them of their tribal obligations and subordinate role to the elders while also celebrating their leadership qualities as new members of the business council.[22] Many tribal members consider the Eagle Drum the foundation of tribal social and ceremonial life still.[23]

What Washington saw as the "official" governing body of Tribes, first in the chiefs and subchiefs, and then in the Joint Business Council which replaced them, was only one of the formal governing bodies of the Tribes. Superimposed upon these secular entities and exerting influence upon them in subtle but powerful ways were the various religious and ceremonial elders of the Tribes, especially in the Arapaho Tribe.

IMPORTANT TIMES FOR THE TRIBAL COUNCIL

The tribal councils on the Wind River Reservations began to come of age, politically speaking, in the middle years of the 1900s. In these years, from approximately 1925 to 1955, the individual business councils and the Joint Business Council proved successful in negotiating many needed agreements and services for tribal constituents. These included important victories in the regulation of oil and gas leases on the reservation, claims against the United States for violation of treaty agreements for both Tribes, the distribution of per capita payments of tribal income previously held in trust by the federal government, and the defeat of attempts to terminate federal aid to the Wind River Tribes. Economic development became a concern of councils in these years, along with

---

22   Fowler, 149-151.
23   Haas Interview.

protection and control of tribal resources.

LAND

During this general period, the question of the legality of the Northern Arapaho presence on the Shoshone Reservation finally came to a head. In 1928, Congress passed a law allowing the Eastern Shoshone Tribe to sue the U.S. government for violating provisions of the The Fort Bridger Treaty of 1868, under which the Eastern Shoshone bands had given up a reservation of more than 44 million acres for exclusive rights to a 3-million-acre reservation on Wind River (see Chapter 2).

George Tunison, attorney for the tribe, argued that without Shoshone approval, the Indian Bureau had allowed the Arapaho to settle permanently at the Shoshone Agency in 1878. From that point on, the government treated both tribes—unofficially and, the Shoshones argued, illegally—as equal beneficiaries of resources, with Arapahos sharing in Shoshone payments from the land cessions of 1896 and 1905, and taking up individual land allotments under the Dawes-Act system.

The case took years to move through federal courts. In 1937, the U.S. Supreme Court finally ruled in the Shoshones' favor. Arapaho people, historian Loretta Fowler writes, were relieved. "They had long smarted under Shoshone accusations of trespass." Now, they could no longer be seen as intruders. Their presence on the reservation was affirmed by the court—and the Shoshones would be compensated for having shared their reservation for six decades. The Shoshone now had to recognize the Arapaho right to live on Wind River and the name of the reservation was officially changed to the Wind River Agency.

The Shoshones were awarded a $4.5 million dollar judgment (more than $87 million in 2024 dollars) and part of the settlement terms were that a portion of the judgment money was to be used to buy back land. The Joint Business Council of the two tribes

Northern Arapaho (back row) and Eastern Shoshone (front row) business councils, 1937. Wyoming State Archives.

began during this period to buy back as much ceded land as they could. The Arapaho, who were not entitled to any monies from the court case, borrowed $500,000 from the Shoshone tribe in order to participate fully in this undertaking. Though many tribe members were initially opposed to the plan, both tribes ultimately benefited from the increase in reservation acreage. By 1940, more than one million acres had been returned to tribal ownership under the land purchase program. This settlement was known as the Tunison Settlement.

In 1955, the Arapaho tribe, in conjunction with the Cheyenne tribes, brought suit against the United States through the Indian Claims Commission for violation of the Fort Laramie Treaty of 1851. The tribes held that they had not been rightfully paid for homelands lost to non-Indians in parts of Wyoming, Colorado, Kansas, and Nebraska. This claim was granted in 1961, bringing the Northern Arapaho on the Wind River Reservation a one quarter share in the settlement. The actual award monies were claimed by the U.S. government as reimbursement for its

1940s payment to the Shoshone tribe for the Arapaho half of the Wind River Reservation. Thus, the Arapaho tribe "paid" for their half of the reservation through this settlement.[24]

ECONOMIC DEVELOPMENT

In 1940, the Arapaho Ranch was established on some of the land bought back by the Tribes, with federal rehabilitation funds to cover the cost of livestock and operating expenses for the first year. This ranch is still a major enterprise of the Arapaho Tribe, sprawling across 300,000 acres in the northeast corner of the reservation. The Shoshones lease their portion of the land to the Arapaho Tribe, whose members run the business independently.

The main goal of management at the Arapaho Ranch is to preserve the delicate balance in nature, while keeping alive traditional Native American values. The Ranch is vigilant in its protection of the diversity of species of plants and animals found naturally on the land, ranging from the major predatory species of wolves, grizzly bears, coyotes, and mountain lions, through the large wild ungulate populations of moose, elk, and mule deer, down to the smallest mammals, birds and plant species. Through careful monitoring of wildlife and range conditions, along with proper grazing management, Arapaho Ranch is able to sustain healthy ecosystems where key symbiotic relationships are allowed to flourish. The monitoring of these key symbiotic relationships is just one of the many tools the Arapaho Ranch uses to support its strong belief in the sustainability of Non-Hormonal Natural Grass Fed Certified Ranching.[25]

From 1917 to 1921, federal leases were granted to drill for oil on the reservation, but production was shut down as it became

---

24   Conversations with Robert Spoonhunter and Jeffrey D. Anderson, North American Indian Heritage Center Wind River Reservation, Wyoming, 1991. *WyoHistory.org*; "Holding on to Sovereignty: The Tribes Mix Old Forms with New," February 5, 2019, https://www.wyohistory.org/encyclopedia/holding-sovereignty-tribes-mix-old-forms-new

25   Arapahoe Ranch. www.arapahoranch.com

financially untenable for the oil companies to drill in the area. For over a decade, an uneasy alliance of tribal members and community members from the towns in Fremont County began to advocate for renewed drilling as royalties would help the Tribes generate desperately needed income. The efforts came to fruition and in 1939, the Joint Business Council was at last successful in pressuring Congress and the BIA to allow the reopening and modification of leases on the Maverick Springs oil field; since then, the Tribes have realized considerable royalty income from oil, gas, and other mineral resources on the reservation.[26]

PER CAPITA PAYMENTS AND TERMINATION EFFORTS

The Business Councils (and eventually the Joint Business Councils) over the years from 1927 to 1947 were gradually successful in getting per capita payments for individual Shoshone and Arapaho tribal members, something they had been trying to do since the early days of the Council. Though Congress had authorized royalty payments from reservation leases to the Tribes in 1924 and 1927, a mechanism for distribution of cash per capita payments was not approved until 1947, and then only for a five-year probationary trial period.

It is important to recall that per capita payments are not a "government dole" but are monies from tribal income distributed to individual tribal members, analogous to stock dividends from the tribe to its "stockholders", the individual tribal members. Each Tribe on the Wind River Reservation receives half of this "trust" income at any given time. A special federal law makes 15% of the income available to each business council and distributes the remaining 85% on a per capita basis to individual

---

26   Judit Olah, "Empowering through Entrepreneurship: The Maverick Springs Oil Field and the Wind River Reservation," (paper presented at the 2007 annual meeting of the Business History Conference, Cleveland, Ohio, June 1-2, 2007), *Business and Economic History On-Line:* https://thebhc.org/sites/default/files/olah.pdf

tribal members. The funds are first divided between each Tribe on a 50-50 basis. Then, those funds are distributed to individuals. Because there are more Arapaho members than Shoshone members, the per capita payments to Arapaho members are lower than those distributed to Shoshone members. This system recognizes that each Tribe is its own sovereign government which shares equally in reservation-wide resources.

With this successful negotiation by the Joint Business Council for two-thirds of tribal income to be distributed in per capita cash payments to individual tribe members, federal welfare, or cash assistance, payments to reservation families, which had been high in the 1940s, were substantially reduced as the per capita was counted as a tribal member's income. There remains a lot of confusion on the part of non-Indians as these per capita payments are not "welfare" payments.

However, conditions on the reservation were far from good with annual incomes of Indian families averaging about $1,200 in the early 1950s.[27] This was far below the average income of non-Indians in the Riverton and Lander areas and meant living from hand to mouth for many families. Per capita payments, upon which many tribe families depended for subsistence, averaged approximately $550 per enrolled Arapaho for an entire year in the ten years after their first distribution in 1947.[28] As previously discussed, the payments to Shoshones were somewhat higher, because there were fewer Shoshones than Arapahos, making each member's share greater.

The Joint Business Council continued to lobby Congress and the Department of the Interior for the continuation and increase in percentage of total tribal income allowed for these vital payments, but the Department of the Interior determined that federal aid and government services and programs to the

27   Records of the BIA, Wind River Reservation, Wyoming.
28   Ibid.

reservations should be terminated before any such increase in per capita payment totals could be granted. This effort at "termination" of the tribes, began in 1953 and was successful on many reservations around the nation.

The concept began in the years after World War II, when a conservative Republican Congress was in power. They looked for ways to cut federal budgets and reduce some of the impact of New Deal programs of the previous era. Wyoming Republican Congressman William Henry Harrison introduced a resolution in the House, outlining the philosophy of termination in June of 1953, saying all of all the tribes in California, Florida, New York, and Texas should be "freed from federal supervision and control"[29] "Termination" meant that the federal recognition of a tribe as a sovereign entity and the federal "trust" responsibility to a tribe and its members, would end.

In response to this policy, the BIA began a voluntary urban relocation program where tribal members could move from their terminated reservation in a rural undeveloped area to a metropolitan area such as Chicago, Denver, Los Angeles, Cleveland, or Seattle. Numerous Native Americans made the drastic move and struggled to adjust to life in a metropolis, facing unemployment, low-end jobs, discrimination, homesickness, and the loss of their traditional cultural support systems. This urban relocation program was disastrous for many of the tribal members who participated. Commonly referred to as the era of "termination and relocation," this period was devastating for many tribes–primarily targeting tribes that were considered to be the most economically successful, often due to valuable natural resources, as the government believed they could assimilate into mainstream society more easily.

The Tribes of Wind River were not an immediate target for

---

29   House Concurrent Resolution No. 108,67, Statute B1 32.

CONSEQUENCES OF FEDERAL TERMINATION POLICIES, 1947-48

Allowed for state jurisdiction over Indians for the first time

Ended the trust relationship between the federal government and some tribes

Raised anew questions of Indian sovereignty

termination, but congress was still looking for ways to cut funding so Congressman Harrison and tribal attorneys negotiated other ways to make tribal members there more independent from federal obligations. This opened the door for the Joint Business Council to win approval for release of 80 percent of tribal income to per capita payments, an increase from the former 66 percent. In 1959, per capita payment to the Tribes went up five percentage points, to 85 percent of all tribal income (payable monthly), where they have remained. As noted earlier, the remaining fifteen percent is used to fund and administer many tribal programs and governing expenses.

For many tribal members, this per capita payment supplements their existing income, and for others it makes up the majority of their livelihood. As previously noted, these per capita payments are not a substitute for payments mandated by treaty obligations, nor are they federal government "welfare." They derive from the royalties of the minerals extracted on reservation land and are dependent on market prices and volatility.

The effort to "terminate" the reservation peoples from federal financial obligations continued, and many bills were introduced and passed in Congress reducing federal sponsorship and services to the tribes. Health care and education, for example, were transferred out of the scope of BIA responsibility.

In 1954, a special Congressional committee released a report recommending the termination of Shoshone and Arapaho Tribes. The Joint Business Council sent long-serving Arapaho councilwoman, Nell Scott, and Shoshone councilman, Bob Harris, to Washington to convince Congress that neither Tribe

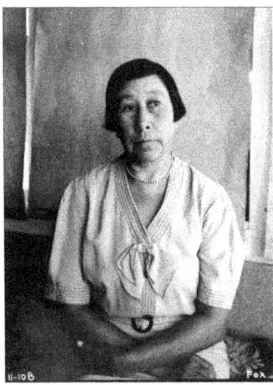

Nell Scott. Chittim Collection,
Jackson Hole Historical Society
and Museum.

Bob Harris (left).
Wyoming State Archives.

was able to do without federal assistance.[30]

Though the total number of terminated tribes in the nation was not high due to treaty commitments and political resistance on the part of the tribes and their supporters, the effect of this termination era was to put a damper on the spirit of reorganization and reform initiated during the Collier administration.

Finally, in 1958, the termination era came to a close with the establishment of a policy of no termination without tribal consent. Termination had been an embarrassing political failure for the Republican administrations of those years. Though the 1953 resolution articulating the philosophies of termination was not officially rescinded until 1970, it was never paid more than lip service during the Kennedy and Johnson administrations of the 1960s.

President Richard M. Nixon formally ended the policy of termination, saying in a speech to Congress in July of 1970:

Because termination is morally and legally unacceptable, because it produces bad practical results, and because the

---

30   Fowler, 210.

> *mere threat of termination tends to discourage greater self sufficiency among Indian groups, I am asking the Congress to pass a new Concurrent Resolution which would expressly renounce, repudiate, and repeal the termination policy.*[31]

The resolution requested by President Nixon passed, but effects of the termination policy upon Indians were felt nevertheless. In general, the policy made the ongoing struggle to preserve important aspects of Indian culture and lifestyle once again extremely difficult, in contrast to the spirit of reform following the 1934 IRA, which fostered a more positive climate of Indian self-governance and preservation of heritage.

In addition, several serious consequences resulted from the termination policy, including the end of absolute exemption from state jurisdiction, the discontinuance of many special federal programs to Indians, the end of the trust relationship between some tribes and the U.S. government, and a challenge to the notion of tribal sovereignty which continues in much of Indian/U.S. government dealings today.[32]

RESTRICTION OF TRIBAL ENROLLMENT

With the awarding of per capita payments came a need for more attention to tribal enrollment standards. Previously, blood heritage was not necessarily required or monitored. Acceptance of tribal ways and culture was often sufficient to guarantee enrollment. The Indian Agent or Superintendent kept tribal rolls until the Tribal Council assumed the responsibility of determining criteria. Gradually, over the years from 1947 on, enrollment criteria tightened so that the Tribes had some control over distribution of per capita payments. Membership for monetary gain was

---

31   Deloria, 20.
32   C.Г. Wilkinson, and E.R. Biggs, "The Evolution of the Termination Policy," *American Indian Law Review,* 139, No. 5 (1977), 90-95.

discouraged. The Tribes consider 1956 the 'base roll' for determining eligibility. Criteria for tribal membership are complicated and still of major concern among Wind River Indians today.

THE COMMITTEE FUNCTION IN TRIBAL GOVERNMENT

In addition to the business councils, social committees became an important part of tribal government as it developed at Wind River over the middle years of the 1900s. These committees organized and coordinated tribal social functions and celebrations, such as pow wows, Christmas parties, and other tribal activities. Some were tasked with economic development.

Today, both tribes still elect an Entertainment Committee of six members each (now called the Tribal Committee by the Arapaho). The committees are responsible for upkeep of community halls, pow wow grounds, and other tribal social activities for each tribe throughout the year. These committees are considered to be very important to the overall functioning of tribal government, coordinating, as they do, some of the tribes' most important ritual and social observances.

SUMMARY

Many changes were effected in tribal government as the business council system evolved on the Wind River Reservation and as national policies were enacted and supplanted over the decades.

A system of checks and balances evolved between 1930 and 1960 between the social committees of the tribes and the political roles of the Joint Business Council, the courts (See Chapter 5) and the general councils. Each was invested with authority and served to balance the power of the other. The authority of Bureau of Indian Affairs' superintendents and their staffs also served as a major check on the authority of the business council members. Many programs and services of the Tribes and the BIA became highly integrated over the years.

Nevertheless, the business councils from 1930 forward wielded considerably more power than the councils of the early 1900s and functioned in a more similar way to American representative democracy than ever before. By 1956, authority over land, mineral leasing, and per capita payments were the Joint Business Council's responsibility.

An important part of the evolution of traditional tribal government was the progression from the primarily mediational/judicial roles of tribal chiefs or elders to the more legislative and executive roles performed by today's business councils. The councils are increasingly involved in policy setting, administration of tribal affairs, and legislation on behalf of the Tribes.

Typical council duties include the administration of tribal contracts, hiring and supervision of staff and program personnel, operation of tribal business enterprises, handling of tribal finances, and the passage of laws and ordinances for the benefit of the Tribes. In the Shoshone Tribe, the business council is no longer empowered to enact legislation. This power is reserved for the Shoshone General Council. Historically, however, both Tribes have authorized their business councils to enact legislation and the Arapaho Tribe has developed a substantial Northern Arapaho Code. (See Chapter 5 for more discussion.)

Though Native American philosophies of governing have been retained in many respects, much of the structure and procedure of council government on the Wind River Reservation closely resembles the political forms of the larger American culture.

For Further Reading:

Fowler, Loretta. *Arapahoe Politics, 1851–1978: Symbols in Crises of Authority*. University of Nebraska Press, 1982.

Hipp, Martha Louise. *Sovereign Schools: How Shoshones and Arapahos Created a High School on the Wind River Reservation*. Bison Books, 2019.

Stamm IV, Henry E. *People of the Wind River: The Eastern Shoshones, 1825–1900*. University of Oklahoma Press, 1999.

O'Gara, Geoffrey. *What You See in Clear Water: Indians, Whites, and a Battle over Water in the American West*. Vintage Departures, 2002.

Chapter 5

MODERN TRIBAL GOVERNMENT

Indian governments today, across the nation and on the Wind River Reservation, reflect both the larger American culture and their own distinctly native cultures and customs. They are unique from any other American political group in some of their political forms, concepts of justice, organizational values, and sovereign rights. One tribe does not mirror the political forms and cultural expressions of another, though there are similarities among native peoples common to all. They have typically increased in both sophistication and formality of political systems over the years, though not always, and many have adopted the governmental structures of the larger culture, with three distinct branches of government: executive, legislative and judicial.

They exist as political groups distinct from the rest of American political life, yet inextricably bound up in the mainstream of it as well. Interaction among the federal government, the states, and Indian tribes continues to confound and perplex Indian and non-Indian leaders alike, resulting in an accumulation of Supreme Court case law which

KEY NAMES AND TERMS

- John Marshall
- McIntosh vs. Johnson
- Domestic dependent nations
- Cherokee Nation cases
- Worcester doctrine
- Plenary power
- Commerce Clause
- Federal trust status
- Sovereignty
- Civil justice
- Restitution
- Advocate
- Limited sovereignty
- Treaty clause
- CFR courts

guides and changes the relationship among the three political entities. As the world and its resources shrink, the importance of understanding tribal government and its relationship to state and federal governments increases, as does the need to live together harmoniously.

FEDERAL POWER OVER TRIBES AND THE CONCEPT OF SOVEREIGNTY

Federal courts have been the main avenue of interpretation of federal and state power over Indian tribes. Such power over the tribes is not specifically granted in the constitution, except in one place, and then only very generally. Called the "Commerce Clause", Article I, Section 8, Clause 3 of the U.S. Constitution gives Congress the power to regulate trade with Indian tribes.

The President is also given power to make treaties with Indian tribes and others in the "Treaty Clause", Article II, Section 2, Clause 2, with ratification of any such treaties by the Senate necessary for final approval, but this treaty power does not imply sovereignty over the tribes. If anything, it implies that Indian tribes and the United States have equal sovereignty, as with foreign nations.

The federal government's power over Indian tribes has been justified as the natural result of military conquest (winner takes all) or as a consequence of the trust (legal guardianship) status the government maintains over the tribes. Actually, the trust status of the federal government, which charges it with upholding treaty obligations and protecting the Indians, should ideally work to preserve limited tribal sovereignty under the terms of many treaties, rather than to usurp it. Unfortunately, as history has shown, this has not often been the case, as treaty after treaty has been violated by the government.

Precedent and practice in Indian law and government can best be understood by the student of Indian government through a review of the court cases which have defined it.

McIntosh vs. Johnson, a case heard by the Supreme Court in 1823, was the first major attempt by the Supreme Court to define the relationship of the federal government to Indian tribes. In it, Chief Justice John Marshall affirmed that Indian tribes were separate political/governmental bodies from the U.S. government, but he also said that discovery and conquest of the tribes by U.S. forces gave the U.S. government the right to full title of Indian land.

In 1831, Marshall again had to rule on the federal-tribe relationship in *Cherokee Nation vs. Georgia*. In this ruling, Marshall granted the Indians of the United States a limited sovereignty as "domestic dependent nations"[1] who were under the guardianship of the federal government. Though they were not as sovereign as independent foreign nations, the Court held that they were legitimate political bodies capable of governing their own internal affairs and of entering into agreements with the federal government.

One year later, this notion of limited sovereignty was further reinforced in the case of *Worcester v. Georgia*, in which the Court defended the Cherokee tribe's right to resist the infringement of Georgia state law within reservation boundaries.

From this case comes the Worcester doctrine, the root of many legal claims to inherent sovereignty of Indian tribes. Its basic premise is that an Indian tribe constitutes a distinct political community. Though Congress has the right to limit or abolish tribal government, the states cannot intrude upon the self-government of tribes unless Congress authorizes it, or a tribe grants permission.

The Cherokee Nation cases established two major precedents in relation to the notion of sovereignty, or which government

---

1   United States Supreme Court, *Cherokee Nation v. Georgia*, 30 U.S. (5 Pet.) I, 1831.

reigns supreme. Clearly, through Justice Marshall's assertions in *Cherokee vs. Georgia*, the idea of the federal government's supremacy over the tribes was articulated: Because the tribes are under the protection of the federal government, they are without complete and independent sovereignty. The second Cherokee Nation case, *Worcester v. Georgia*, held that the tribes did have enough sovereignty to be immune from state governance (except where provided for by Congress).[2]

Of course, many other tests and assertions by both government and tribal representatives over the years have put differing spins on the degree to which the tribes are, or should be, considered sovereign nations. The subject is still a matter for serious debate and legal challenge. But the current reality is that in practice, the federal government does reign supreme over the tribes. Congress, the legislative branch of the U.S. government, has plenary power over the tribes–that is, complete and absolute authority to regulate tribal matters and even to recognize or abolish a tribe.

The right of the tribes to use their sovereignty to resist state interference is also generally true in practice, though less clearly. There have been many cases and laws which have altered this relationship between the states and the tribes, the most notable of which, Public Law 280, passed in 1953, is the only law passed by Congress which imposes significant state jurisdiction on some reservations.[3]

The General Allotment Act of 1887 and many laws passed during the termination period (1950-1968) indirectly gave states more jurisdiction over tribes by opening up tribal lands for purchase (and control) and by encouraging the dissolution of communal tribal property and systems of traditional government. Indeed, during the termination period, laws were passed which resulted in

2   Deloria, 33.
3   Pevar, 103.

the termination of more than 100 tribes by the federal government.[4] Other laws have been passed which apply to specific tribes or states in limiting sovereignty of the tribes. Nevertheless, in general, the federal courts of the nation have held firm in the notion that tribes are not under the governance of states.

It is important to remember that many Indians are not in agreement with the federal interpretation of Indian sovereignty, as manifested in the Supreme Court decisions or executive policies, nor do all Indians agree among themselves on the issue. Some believe that sovereignty cannot be granted by some other power, but that supreme power comes only from spiritual sources. And some believe sovereignty is granted to rulers by consent of the governed. Sovereignty is commonly defined as that power and quality of independence nations have which entitles them to govern themselves.[5]

Total and complete political, social, and economic independence from other states or countries is probably not possible in this day and age, for the tribes or any nation in the world. The notion of complete self-determination for tribes (where the BIA would be abolished) is not without difficulty for many Indians, because though it promotes Indian autonomy, it also implies the loosening of federal bonds in the trust relationship. That discontinuation of guardianship by the federal government is seen as a threat to Indian survival by some.

The concept of sovereignty is, at best, a qualified one signifying a complex relationship among federal, state, and tribal governments which will continue to evolve and change with the political and economic conditions of the times.

---

4   Pevar, 107-8.
5   *Tribal Political Systems: Laws, Treaties and Government* (Spearfish, South Dakota: Black Hills State College Centre of Indian Studies, 1972). 132-144.

INHERENT POWERS OF TRIBES

Though not all issues of sovereignty are clear or settled, the Supreme Court has long recognized certain inherent powers of all Indian tribes to govern themselves with respect to certain matters. The major areas of tribal authority are the right to form a government, the right to determine membership, the right to tax, the right to maintain justice, the right to regulate domestic relations (such as marriage and divorce), and the right to regulate commerce and trade. These are the same general powers held by state and federal governments, with some exceptions.

STATE OF WYOMING

The State of Wyoming has the same basic legal relationship to the Tribes on the Wind River Reservation as all states generally, as outlined in the federal definitions of state and tribal authority noted above. Because Wyoming did not choose to assert its authority under PL-280 (and now, no state may do so without tribal consent), Supreme Court cases that interpret state and tribal authority under PL-280 do not usually apply in Wyoming. There are also a number of specific legal rulings that limit or define state authority, if any, on the Wind River Reservation. For example, tribal water rights have been quantified on behalf of the Tribes and Wyoming must honor those rights. The right to offer casino-style Indian gaming in Wyoming also has been determined by the courts (see Chapter 6). Wyoming has agreements in place with the Tribes to fund child protection services and to exempt fuel and tobacco taxes on sales to tribal members. Wyoming has several state statutes that affect the relationship with the Tribes, including one providing "full faith and credit" to most Tribal Court judgements, making them more readily enforceable outside the Reservation. The Wyoming Legislature has a tribal relations committee that considers ways for state law to help resolve conflicts between the tribal and state governments.

INHERENT POWERS OF TRIBES
Right to form a government
Right to determine membership
Right to tax
Right to maintain law and order
Right to regulate property
Right to regulate commerce and trade

There is one section of the Wyoming State Constitution which specifically deals with Indian relations. Article 21, Section 26 proclaims that Wyoming citizens "forever disclaim all right and title...to all land owned or held by an Indian or Indian tribes, and until the title thereto shall have been extinguished by the United States, the same shall be and remain subject to the disposition of the United States...under absolute jurisdiction and control of the congress of the United States..."[6] Essentially, the state constitution concedes what was already true as a matter of federal law, that only the U.S. can extinguish or take title to Indian trust lands–the title to which is held by the U.S. in trust for the tribe or tribal member–against the will of the tribe or tribal member.

SELF-DETERMINATION

In the years after the termination period, federal policy toward Indians shifted again, back towards the self-determination goals of the reorganization years of the 1930s and 1940s, in which emphasis had been placed on Indian autonomy and self-government. In 1968, President Lyndon B. Johnson announced a new goal in Indian policy, one ending once and for all the lingering debate about termination and stressing instead the goals of tribal self-determination.

In 1970, President Richard M. Nixon, who had been vice president during part of the termination era, reinforced his predecessor's stand on Indian policy saying: "This, then, must be

---

6   Wyoming State Constitution, Article 21, Section 26, pp. 59-60. Published by the Secretary of State's Office, 1988.

the goal of any new national policy toward the Indian people: to strengthen the Indian sense of autonomy without threatening his sense of community."[7]

One of the primary pieces of legislation passed by Congress during this period was the Indian Civil Rights Act. In addition to conferring most Constitutional civil rights upon persons subject to the jurisdiction of tribal governments, states were prohibited from exercising jurisdiction over tribes without their express consent. This important amendment to the provisions of Public Law 280, which had given states first-time-ever jurisdictional powers over certain tribes, restored in part the sovereign status of tribes in relation to state governments. As noted above, when PL-280 was enacted, states that wanted certain criminal or civil jurisdiction in Indian country had to opt-in or assert that authority. Wyoming did not do so and has never been a "PL-280 state," but the Indian Civil Rights Act was an important declaration of the rights of tribes.

Other social legislation was enacted in the late 1960s and early 1970s which emphasized tribal self-determination. The Indian Financing Act and the Native American Programs Act, passed in 1974, assisted tribes in developing tribal resources more effectively.[8] Both Tribes of the Wind River Reservation used funding from the Indian Financing Act to support local businesses and entrepreneurship and the development of tourism initiatives. The Native American Programs Act created the Administration for Native Americans (ANA), an agency within the department of Health and Human Services, to fund social and economic development projects, language preservation, and educational programs. The ANA funded various projects on the Wind River Reservation, including language revitalization, and

---

7   President Richard M. Nixon, Message, "Recommendations of Indian Policy," (Government Printing Office: Washington, D.C., 1970).
8   Pevar, 7.

initiatives to improve social services and infrastructure on the reservation.

The Indian Self Determination and Education Assistance Act of 1975 provided for qualifying tribes and certain Indian organizations to administer federal Indian programs on reservations. This gave the tribes, rather than the BIA, the power to decide upon their participation in some federal programs. It also required the BIA (and certain other federal agencies that served tribal members) to contract with tribal governments to provide those services instead, using federal funds (often referred to as "638" contracts).

Though many looked upon the programs of President Johnson's "Great Society" as being new in relation to Indians, they were, in fact, a resurrection of spirit of 1934 IRA reforms, which had never fully come to pass, partly because of the intervening termination policies.

ONGOING ISSUES OF SOVEREIGNTY AND JURISDICTION

Periodic court battles are entered into by the Tribes in such matters as who has legal jurisdiction over crimes committed (the state, the Tribes, or the federal government), water, land, mineral resource issues, taxation, and regulation of commerce. Sometimes these legal cases have major implications for the people of the reservation.

THE COBELL CASE

This case began at the national level but has an extraordinary impact on local tribes. The *Cobell* case was a very important legal case that involved Native American land and money. It started in 1996 and was named after Elouise Cobell, a Blackfeet woman who wanted the U.S. government to return money owed to Native Americans. Officially known as *Cobell v. Salazar*, the case was a class-action lawsuit filed in 1996 that focused on the U.S. government's mismanagement of Native American trust funds. Cobell was a Blackfeet tribal member, banker, and advocate for Native American rights. She led the case to seek justice for Native Americans who had been deprived of money owed to them from land revenues, including resources like oil, gas, timber, and grazing fees. Essentially, the U.S. government mismanaged billions of dollars that should have gone to Native Americans through incomprehensibly poor record-keeping and breaching their fiduciary duty as a trustee with a legal duty to manage the funds responsibly.

The case took thirteen years to wind through the legal system, with one of the main problems being it was nearly impossible to calculate the amount of money the United States owed individual tribal members. In 2009, the case was settled, with the United States agreeing to pay $3.4 billion to pay back individuals, buy back land for reservations and establish a scholarship fund for Native American students. The Cobell case was important because it made the U.S. government take responsibility for its mismanagement of its fiduciary duty.

On the Wind River Reservation, tribal members with Individual Indian Money accounts that had been set up by the government to manage revenue from their lands were partially repaid for years of mismanaged income from land resources like oil, gas, grazing, and timber. Also, part of the Cobell settlement money was used to start the Land Buy-Back Program for Tribal Nations which helped tribes buy back fractionated land parcels from individual landowners. Fractionated lands are pieces of land that have been split up among many individual owners over generations of inheritance, making it difficult to manage or develop. This program allowed the Eastern Shoshone and Northern Arapaho tribes to buy back some of these fractionated lands. By consolidating ownership, the tribes gained more control over reservation lands, which helped with land management and opened up more opportunities for economic development, such as leasing land for agriculture, housing, or energy development.

However, the program did not cover all the fractionated lands on the Wind River Reservation and now, a generation later, these unconsolidated parcels have fractionated even further and contribute to the extremely complex and fragmented nature of land ownership on the reservation. In what is frequently called the "checkerboard" map of land ownership, you will find tribal land owned by the Eastern Shoshone or Northern Arapaho tribes, individual Native land owned by individual Native Americans, and land owned by non-Indians. These lands break down into *trust land, fee land,* and *allotted land.*

Trust land is land held in trust by the U.S. government for the benefit of the tribes or individual Native Americans. The U.S. government technically owns the title but holds it for the exclusive benefit of the tribe or individual. Tribal trust land is governed by the tribes while individually-owned trust land is still subject to federal oversight. Trust land can't be sold, transferred, or mortgaged without approval from the U.S. government.

Fee land, or "fee simple" land, is privately owned and can be bought, sold, or transferred without federal restrictions. It's not held in trust by the federal government and can be owned by Native Americans, non-Native individuals, corporations, or other entities. Unlike trust land, fee land is subject to state and local property taxes. Ownership of fee land gives the owner full control over the property, including the right to develop, lease, or sell it, often without tribal oversight.

Allotted land refers to parcels of reservation land that were divided and given to individual Native Americans during the federal allotment era, particularly under the Dawes Act of 1887. Allotted land was initially held in trust by the government for a period, after which it could be converted to fee land, though some land remains in trust status today. Many allotted lands have been passed down through generations, and as heirs inherit shares, the land becomes "fractionated," meaning multiple individuals hold shared ownership. This fractionation can lead to dozens or even hundreds of co-owners for a single parcel, each holding a small percentage. Allotted lands that remain in trust have protections similar to other trust lands and cannot be sold or transferred without federal approval. However, fractionated ownership makes decision-making difficult, as all co-owners must agree on leases or uses. This was the issue that the Land Buy-Back Program of the Cobell settlement sought to address, though not all fractionated land was consolidated and these parcels add to the monumental concerns of land management on this checkerboard map of the reservation.

THE YELLOWBEAR BOUNDARY CASE

Land ownership and jurisdiction was also a key issue in what is known as the *Yellowbear Boundary* case. As we have seen, over the years, various federal policies and actions, including land allotments and land cessions (or "land diminishment"), have complicated the reservation's boundaries and raised questions about which government—state, federal, or tribal—has jurisdiction over certain areas.

Andrew Yellowbear, Jr., a Northern Arapaho tribal member, was serving a life sentence in state prison in connection with the 2004 murder of his young daughter in Riverton when, in 2015, after several years of legal wrangling, the Northern Arapaho and Eastern Shoshone tribes won a landmark administrative decision by the Environmental Protection Agency (EPA). The federal agency concluded–with U.S. Justice Department assent–that a million more acres about 100 miles southeast of Jackson belonged to the Tribes. The additional land would increase the reservation's size by nearly one-third and would include the town of Riverton.

The Tribes' stated goal was to set air-pollution standards. But the implications of the EPA decision could be far-reaching, including legal jurisdiction in criminal cases.

The state of Wyoming, along with Riverton officials, challenged the EPA decision, and the matter went to the courts. Yellowbear, who was already seeking to have his case relitigated, filed a "friend of the court" brief in the boundary dispute. He claimed his conviction should be put aside for a new trial in a tribal court since Riverton was now part of the reservation. Yellowbear's case became intertwined with the Tribes' case and drew a lot of attention to the issue. The Northern Arapaho fought to prevent him from joining in their case, and ultimately, a federal appeals court denied Yellowbear's plea to participate in the boundary dispute. In 2017, the 10th U.S. Circuit Court of Appeals sided with Wyoming, ruling that Congress had diminished the reservation's boundaries in the early 20th century, placing Riverton under state, not reservation jurisdiction. This ruling solidified established decisions, as the Wyoming Supreme Court had weighed in numerous times between 1950 and 2008, all supporting the conclusion that a 1905 congressional act had ceded all land north of the Wind River. After the federal court ruled in favor of the state, Yellowbear continued to pursue jurisdictional issues but his case was dismissed in 2020.

WATER ON THE RESERVATION

Water rights cases on the Wind River Reservation involve questions about who has the legal right to use water from rivers, streams, and underground sources on the reservation and how much water they're allowed to use. These cases are important because water is essential for farming, livestock, drinking, and industrial uses, especially in dry regions like Wyoming.

Under a legal principle called the *Winters doctrine* (from a 1908 Supreme Court decision in *Winters v. United States*), Native

American tribes are granted water rights to support their reservations. This includes enough water to fulfill the needs of their people, even if the tribes didn't specifically claim it at the time of the treaty.

One of the most important water rights cases for the Wind River Reservation is known as the Big Horn River Adjudication, which began in 1977. This case aimed to determine the amount of water the tribes were entitled to from the Wind and Big Horn rivers and other water sources on the reservation.

The case took decades, moving through different levels of court and ending up at the U.S. Supreme Court. In 1988, the Wyoming Supreme Court ruled that the tribes did indeed have reserved water rights, based on the Winters Doctrine, but only for water used for agriculture, livestock, and domestic needs.

After affirming that the tribes had reserved water rights, the next step was to quantify, or figure out how much water they were entitled to. The courts ultimately allowed the tribes enough water to support their current and reasonably foreseeable future needs, mainly for irrigation purposes. This is known as the "practicably irrigable acreage" (PIA) standard, which determines water rights based on how much land can feasibly be irrigated.

In 2013, the Eastern Shoshone and Northern Arapaho tribes tried to secure instream flow rights—the right to keep water flowing naturally through rivers and streams to protect fish, wildlife, and natural habitats. Instream flow rights are important for maintaining ecosystems and ensuring sustainable water use.

The state of Wyoming challenged this request, arguing that instream flow was not part of the original water rights granted. In 2016, the Wyoming Supreme Court ruled against the tribes, deciding they couldn't secure these instream flow rights under their reserved water rights.

These water rights battles between the State of Wyoming and the Tribes of the Wind River Reservation have been going on for decades and are further examples of the complex struggles over jurisdiction. Today, the Tribes have their own Water Code, which establishes the Tribal Water Engineer office, but many questions remain about who will manage and fund these efforts, and about other water-related issues on the reservation.

HERRERA V. WYOMING

Another example of tribal jurisdiction and boundary concerns is the *Herrera v. Wyoming* case. In January 2014, Clayvin Herrera, a member of the Crow Tribe, hunted elk in Bighorn National Forest in Wyoming. This hunting, which took place outside the Crow Reservation, led to his legal case after Wyoming charged him with violating state hunting laws. Herrera argued that he was exercising his treaty right, established in the 1868 Fort Laramie Treaty which allowed the Crow Tribe to hunt on "unoccupied lands of the United States" in perpetuity.

Wyoming countered that the treaty right was invalidated when Wyoming became a state in 1890, as the doctrine of *equal footing* implied that states gain full control over resources within their borders upon statehood. The state thus contested the *Worcester v. Georgia* doctrine by challenging the scope of Native American treaty rights on state lands, particularly regarding hunting rights outside reservation boundaries. Wyoming's stance suggested that state sovereignty and authority over natural resources, as established through statehood, could supersede treaty rights. This position, if upheld, would weaken *Worcester's* protections by allowing states to assert jurisdiction over Native treaty rights without federal intervention.

The U.S. Supreme Court ruled in favor of Herrera in 2019, reaffirming that the Crow Tribe's hunting rights under the 1868 treaty had not been extinguished by Wyoming's statehood. The decision reinforced the *Worcester* doctrine by emphasizing that Native American treaty rights remain federally protected and are not automatically overridden by state interests or statehood. This case ultimately reaffirmed the principle that states cannot unilaterally infringe on treaty rights held by tribes.

These cases illustrate the complex legal issues that the Tribes' councils must contend with as they govern. Chapter 6 goes into great detail about the complex inter-governmental issues and the protracted legal maneuvers on the part of the State of Wyoming as the Wind River Tribes sought to develop the reservation economy through legalized gaming. In addition to the standard roles of governance, the processes to protect and serve the people of the reservation, issues of sovereignty, self-determination, and jurisdiction make the job of governing much more challenging.

TODAY'S BUSINESS COUNCILS

Each tribe at Wind River still has its own tribal council, called a Business Council, composed of six members. Shoshone Business Council members are elected for four-year terms in a staggered rotation. Arapaho Business Council members are elected for two-year terms. Each council appoints a chair and vice- or co-chairperson. Regular meetings of each tribe's Business Council are held separately but the two Tribes also come together in an inter-tribal council, chaired by the leaders of the Shoshone and Arapaho councils on a rotating basis. Additionally, members of the inter-tribal council serve on several different subcommittees, ranging from land resources to health and welfare to tax issues, which study and recommend action in specific areas.

As noted before, the BIA historically has pushed for both Tribes to act as one, through a single inter-tribal council. Nonetheless, each Tribe has its own history, language, treaties, membership rules, and sovereignty. When they choose to act together, they have often used an inter-tribal council approach. Prior to 2016, they acted through the "Joint Business Council" (JBC).

Problems and disagreements between the tribes often left matters under the JBC in limbo or ineffective. "Joint" programs often divided federal resources between the tribes on a 50-50 basis, resulting in fewer dollars and inferior services provided to members of the more numerous Northern Arapaho Tribe (NAT). For example, in 1996, the NAT negotiated with the U.S. housing program (HUD) to fund a NAT housing authority, separate and apart from the joint Wind River Housing Authority. The newly founded NAT program would provide much needed housing for NAT members and would supplement the on-going joint program. The Eastern Shoshone Tribe (EST) filed a federal lawsuit against NAT on the grounds that the Shoshone and Arapaho Law & Order Code (joint code) established the joint housing authority and the code could only be amended with the consent of both Tribes. In other words, EST claimed that NAT could not act independently to gain federal contracts for services to NAT members. The NAT said it was merely exercising its own sovereign authority. The federal court dismissed the lawsuit, and the joint housing program eventually dissolved. EST then created its own, separate housing authority to serve members of the EST.

Problems with the Joint Business Council system erupted again in 2014, when NAT dissolved the JBC and resolved to act cooperatively with EST through existing joint committees instead.[9] The BIA resisted efforts by NAT to contract separately for certain services. A lawsuit by NAT against the BIA was resolved when the two business councils re-organized the joint council into what is now called the Inter-Tribal Council.

Each business council is said to derive its power and authority from its separate general council, the absolute authority of each tribe, made up of all adult tribe members. However, as previously

---

9   County 10, a local online news source, published the September 9, 2014, letter at the time to NAT members explaining the dissolution; http://county10. com/2014/09/10

discussed in Chapter 1, the BIA recognizes each business council, not each general council. General council meetings are held a few times a year as needed. Such things as conditions for tribal enrollment, gaming issues, and management of fish and game on the reservation are reserved for these general council dealings.

Additionally, any matter not *traditionally* handled by the business council usually must come before the Tribe as a whole. This is a result of the Tribes' decision not to draw up and ratify constitutions for their individual Tribes, which would have spelled out specific responsibilities of each governing body and provided structure for continuing tribal governance.

In the last few years, business council members have initiated the practice of holding informational meetings of the general councils, in addition to regular general council meetings to share more fully the daily deliberations of the business council and to facilitate adequate discussion of major tribal concerns. Otherwise, as one councilman put it, "We are asking the General Council to hear and decide an issue in 30 minutes, when it has taken us three months to figure it out." As complexity of government grows on the reservation, business council members feel the responsibility to educate their fellow tribe members more fully in major issues confronting them.

The Indian Reorganization Act of 1934 (IRA), also known as the Wheeler-Howard Act, provided to the tribes of the United States the opportunity to re-organize under constitutions that subjected tribal authority to approval by the federal government. Though intended in some ways to reduce the influence of the dependence on the Bureau of Indian Affairs and the Congress, many tribes were glad they did not re-organize under the Act. The Wind River tribes rejected its terms and the days since this New Deal program have meant continued gains in strength of tribal government, as well as a larger voice in dealing with the federal government. Many of the reforms of the IRA, such as tribal courts, have been adopted by the Wind River Tribes, even though they rejected the constitutional option of Wheeler-Howard.

It has also meant that Indian government, for better or worse, has grown to more closely resemble the government of the larger U.S. culture. The formerly abhorrent idea of holding a primary before the general election, for example, a reform urged by agency superintendents 40 years earlier, was adopted as standard practice in 1972 by the Arapaho Tribe. Arapaho candidates since that time have been required to register to be in the primary, the top 12 being selected as final candidates for the six council positions to be determined by the general election, held in November. The Shoshone Tribe did not hold primary elections until 1990. Prior to that, it was not uncommon for as many as 50 candidates to be nominated and voted on in the general election.

Another key change in the council is increasing political and legal sophistication. Both the Shoshone and Arapaho council members are more politically aware than in early years and more in tune with what is required in a predominantly White political world. More and more, each business council relies on the guidance and expertise of tribal attorneys prior to acting on tribal matters. In earlier times, appeals to the federal government were the only recourse the Tribes had, and their political clout was at times questionable. Today, the Tribes wield considerable, though perhaps not adequate, power.

The Inter-Tribal Business Council still gets much of its direction from the BIA in many tribal business matters, but the power and influence of the BIA over ITBC proceedings is less than in the formative years of the council. Many Indians and political scholars believe that the BIA has outlived its usefulness to tribes and will eventually be replaced by newer, less bureaucratic systems representing the federal government as Indian tribes decrease their dependence on the government.[10]

However, others feel that reorganization and reform of BIA policies and bureaucracy is a better answer to current problems than abolishing the BIA-tribe relationship altogether. They point out that a major advantage of maintaining the BIA is that it is well-established in Washington and on the reservations, a recognized political entity with a relatively predictable funding level. Many believe that adoption of self-governing relationships by the tribes, where they would contract directly with the federal government for services, would place tribes in serious jeopardy for funding.

Some tribal leaders maintain that direct management of the tribes by the BIA is a safer way of protecting tribal interests for the future. The trust responsibility of the United States government, established under terms of the treaties with the tribes, includes the responsibility to help Indians preserve the health and welfare of the tribes. Independence from such trust responsibility conjures up images in the minds of some tribal members of the disastrous days of termination, when many Indian tribes, attempting to be more and more self-sufficient, were left "high and dry" by the government as a "reward" for increasing self-sufficiency. The Wind River Tribes, as noted in earlier chapters, narrowly escaped the hardships of termination experienced by many other tribes around the nation. The memory of what they view as a thinly veiled attempt at assimilating the Indian population, once and for all into the larger culture still threatens tribal members at Wind River.

Whatever the faults and tensions between the BIA and the tribes, many see it as still the best solution to management of Indian affairs, current moves towards self-determination

---

10   D. Lester, Executive Director, Council of Energy Resource Tribes (CERT), in an address to Native American State Legislators, (National Conference of State Legislators' Native American Forum, Denver, Colorado, June 28, 1991).

notwithstanding. The largest impediment from removing the BIA completely is that the Tribe and individual tribal members do not hold fee or individual title to trust lands. Those are held in trust by the Department of the Interior with the BIA acting as the trustee.

THE INDIAN JUDICIARY

Long before BIA establishment of tribal councils, traditional tribal justice was handled by the appropriate elders in a tribe. Most tribes were organized around social, religious, and military functions. The resolution of conflict fell to the appropriate elder with the relevant sphere of activity, if that determination could be made. The three areas were not wholly distinct, with much overlap between them, so a clear and precise separation of such powers was not emphasized.[11]

The main goal of traditional tribal justice was to restore harmony to the tribe through careful negotiation with the feuding parties. Judeo-Christian notions of punishment and retribution were not emphasized in original systems of Indian justice, the aim being more to restore each party's dignity and sense of wholeness, with the help of tribe elders. Guilt and innocence, as thought of in the setting of the larger culture of American courtrooms, had little to do with the issue in these traditional "courts." The goal was to ensure that both parties in a dispute came away feeling satisfied. Since offenses against an individual were seen as offenses against an entire extended family, resolution of conflicts between individuals took on heightened importance.

Compensation for harm done, or restitution, was a key component of Indian justice. Even in the case of a serious offense like murder, guilt and punishment were less the goal than satisfactory restitution to the family of the victim. Rather than right and wrong, the key thing to be decided by the parties involved,

11   Ibid.

TRADITIONAL PHILOSOPHIES OF JUSTICE	
NATIVE AMERICAN	**ANGLO-AMERICAN**
Meditational	Adversarial
Social sanctions/restitution	Restitution/punishment
Satisfaction of all parties	Satisfaction of wronged parties
Restoration of tribal harmony	Protection of society
Restoration of self esteem & wholeness to all	Guilt and innocence
	Restoration

with the help of a "judge" (tribal chief, elder, or holy man), was what constituted a fair and satisfactory compromise that would allow the tribe to get on with its affairs peacefully. The traditional judge(s) sometimes even contributed his personal wealth or goods to the restitution, if it meant preserving tribal unity.[12] The most punishing consequence meted out in traditional Indian justice was banishment from the tribe, and this was done only when tribal safety, survival, or values were seriously threatened.

As the councils of tribes around the nation became more involved in policy-making, administration, and legislation on behalf of the tribes, many of the mediating and judicial functions of tribal councils were turned over to other entities. In the late nineteenth century, the Department of the Interior created the Courts of Indian Offenses with the express goal of eliminating elements of Native culture through the coercive power of criminal law. The courts stood on dubious constitutional grounds, they were almost universally replaced by tribal courts in the twentieth century, and they have been widely derided as crude assimilationist tools.[13]

---

12   Deloria, 113.
13   Alexandra Fay, "Courts of Indian Offenses, Courts of Indian Resistance," *Michigan Law Review*, 2026, https://papers.ssrn.com/sol3/papers.cfm?abstract_id=5179380

These Courts of Indian Offenses, also known as CFR courts, because they followed the Code of Federal Regulations, arose between the time of traditional Indian courts and modern day tribal courts. They were sponsored by the BIA in the late 1800s, though the exact range of their jurisdiction was not wholly specified. Most scholars today do not believe they were meant to be courts in the real sense of the term, observing that assimilation and detribalization were the primary purposes of the CFR courts, with protection of Indian rights and peace-keeping only secondary. These CFR courts were not created with any statutory authority but were viewed as a legitimate extension of BIA powers on the reservation.[14] Before the western territories became states, they were the only "local" law and order on the reservation. As states formed and began developing their own codes and laws, the CFR courts began to recognize and reflect individual state laws within CFR ordinances.

The CFR courts were presided over by Indian judges, but BIA agency personnel were careful, especially in the beginning years, to choose Indian judges who were willing to embrace non-Indian ways of thinking about justice. Sometimes, the judges' rulings were even overruled by the reservation agent. These courts were accused of being a form of cultural oppression, particularly in their formative years, since many of the cases they tried involved banning Indian religious dances, ceremonials, and other native traditions.

At one time, CFR courts were present on about two-thirds of the nation's reservations. With the advent of the 1934 Indian Reorganization Act, however, the BIA was discouraged from having this kind of influence over tribal matters and these courts gradually disappeared from most reservations.[15] Today, only a handful remain across the nation.

---

14   Deloria, 115.
15   Ibid.

At Wind River, the CFR court remained in existence until 1987, when the Joint Business Council approved the creation of a tribal court. Tribal ordinances were codified and procedural laws were reviewed and revised. Though the creation of the tribal court system and accompanying Law and Order Code did not change a great deal of the substantive law of the tribe, it did introduce more sophisticated and protective legal procedures to Wind River law. It also broadened the civil jurisdiction of the tribe in significant ways.

Under CFR courts, civil jurisdiction was limited to offenses by or between Indians. The CFR court could also hear a case when just one of the parties was a tribal member *if* the tribal member was the defendant or, if not the defendant, upon agreement by both parties to the action.[16] Though a non-Indian could file an action against an Indian under CFR court, an Indian could not file an action against anyone but other Indians. Tribe members were severely limited in their ability to obtain civil justice on the reservation under this system. (Criminal jurisdiction is federally limited in complicated ways.)

In the current tribal court system, this jurisdiction is expanded to reflect modern legal views; that is, civil jurisdiction has to do with where the civil incident takes place, and not with the ethnicity of persons involved.[17] This change means that issues of taxation, oil and gas lease questions, and many other issues can be heard in tribal courts for the first time.

The broadest generalization which can be made about tribal courts is that they most often deal with civil disputes and minor crimes between Indians who are members of the tribe. Child abuse and offenses related to alcohol and drug abuse are types of criminal cases commonly heard in the tribal court at Wind River.

---

16   William C. Canby, Jr. "Civil Jurisdiction and the Indian Reservation System," *Utah Law Review* 206 (1973).
17   St. Clair Interview.

In criminal cases, there are several important principles and federal statutes which regulate the complicated issue of jurisdiction. In general, the federal government through Congress had the authority to determine who exercises jurisdiction over crimes in Indian country. Tribal courts generally lack criminal jurisdiction over non-Indians, but non-Indians may be subject to regulation and civil fines for violations of tribal law.

However, as summarized in the table on page 137 there is much Congressional legislation to the contrary. The primary statutes which modify Indian criminal jurisdiction are the General Crimes Act, the Major Crimes Act, the Assimilative Crimes Act, parts of the Indian Civil Rights Act of 1968, and Public Law 280. Other principles which are generally true of Indian criminal jurisdiction are that tribal criminal codes do not apply to non-Indians, and the states cannot exercise jurisdiction over Indians on reservations. There are few exceptions to these principles.

The modern tribal courts, then, came into being after the IRA and were designed to help the tribes govern themselves, especially in civil matters, in ways which met their evolving needs. Things like divorce cases, alcohol-related and drug offenses, and child custody disputes are often the subject of tribal court dockets. Criminal matters before the court are usually misdemeanor offenses.

One of the differences between most tribal courts and the Anglo-American court system of state and federal bureaucracies is in the degree of formality observed. Tribal courts, by and large, operate more informally and without as much attention to legal technicalities as do modern American courtrooms. Of course, as tribal courts grow more and more sophisticated and employ judges and advocates trained in Anglo-American jurisprudence, more similar, formal procedures are likely to increase.

In many cases, the judge in a tribal court is not a lawyer. Often a judge is appointed by the tribal council based on his or her judgement, integrity, and respect in the community. In other tribes, the religious leaders select the judges, and in still others, judges are elected by vote of the General Council.

The Shoshone & Arapaho Courts of the Wind River Reservation are Courts of general civil and criminal jurisdiction at both the trial and appellate levels. The Wind River Tribal Court serves the Wind River Reservation and members of the Eastern Shoshone and Northern Arapaho Tribe. The Shoshone and Arapaho Law and Order Code was adopted in 1987 by both tribes. There have been updates and revisions to the code since that time and the Wind River Tribal Court enforces the tribal code.[18]

There are four types of courts on the Wind River Reservation: trial court, probate court (wills and estates), children's court and court of appeals. The judges meet monthly to discuss general procedural concerns and legal questions relating to cases. The chief judge will advise the associates on matters of law if they request such assistance. Agencies who frequently appear in tribal court on behalf of clients (i.e., children's services) are often invited to attend to gain a better understanding of Wind River laws.

One difference between tribal court and state court, at least on the Wind River Reservation, is that clients appearing in tribal court may choose between representation by an attorney or an advocate at their discretion. Advocates are not lawyers, though they must pass the same legal exam administered to tribal associate judges before representing a client. Though the structure and procedure in many tribal courtrooms, including those on the Wind River, increasingly resemble Anglo-American systems, the interpretation and administration of law and order often reflect elements of a distinctly native philosophy of justice.

---

18   *Wind River Tribal Court,* https://www.wrtribalcourt.com/

FEDERAL LEGISLATION AFFECTING TRIBAL JURISDICTION

The General Crimes Act   1854

Said that U.S. laws relating to "punishment of offenses" shall extend to Indian country, except in the case of offenses committed between Indians or by an Indian in Indian country who had already been punished by tribal laws. Also excluded any Indian lands where specific treaty provisions prohibited jurisdiction by the state or federal government.

The Major Crimes Act   1885

Named seven major crimes which the federal government would take jurisdiction over in Indian country. Expanded to include the 14 felonies of murder, manslaughter, kidnapping, rape, carnal knowledge of minor females, assault with intent to commit rape, incest, assault with intent to commit murder, assault with a dangerous weapon, assault resulting in serious bodily injury, arson, burglary, robbery, and larceny.

Took jurisdiction of these major crimes away from tribal government. Motivated by the famous murder of Sioux Chief Spotted Tail by Crow Dog, in which the federal government upheld the Sioux tribe's right to solve the conflict using traditional tribal laws. Spotted Tail's family agreed upon a suitable settlement for the murder, but the non-Indian public was outraged that Crow Dog was not executed or otherwise severely punished for his crime. A campaign was mounted by non-Indian citizenry to transfer control of major crimes out of Indian hands.

The Assimilative Crimes Act   1898

Permitted the federal government to apply state laws to federal enclaves such as reservations where no other specific law exists. Minor criminal offenses can be turned over to state jurisdiction whenever tribal or federal laws do not specifically prohibit it.

Further eroded tribal sovereignty and jurisdiction.

Public Law 280 (PL 280)   1953

Gave criminal and civil jurisdiction on Indian reservations to the states of Alaska, California, Minnesota, Nebraska, Oregon, and Wisconsin, and allowed for other states to amend their constitutions to supersede federal and/or tribal jurisdiction.

Was part of the termination effort of the 1950s. Replaced tribal authority with state authority. Was amended in 1968 to require the consent of tribes first.

The Indian Civil Rights Act   1968

Made many of the provisions in the Bill of Rights applicable to tribal courts, placing further restrictions on the disposition of criminal cases. Included such rights as free speech, protection against double jeopardy, the right to counsel (at defendant's own expense), the right to due process, the protection against self-incrimination, etc.

While these rights protected the individual Indian, they also eroded traditional tribal jurisdiction

Source: The Rights of Indians and Tribes, ACLU, 1983

Punishment and retribution appear to be less important in Wind River tribal court than mediation and assistance, at least in certain kinds of cases. The Northern Arapaho Tribe enacted a Peacemaker system to allow for traditional mediation in certain kinds of cases. So, while the tribal judicial system may parallel the legal procedure of other American courtrooms, its legal philosophy seems to reflect a uniquely Indian set of values.[19]

Tribal court decisions are seldom appealed, though there is a mechanism to allow for that. With power only to levy relatively small fines and impose short jail sentences, and domestic civil cases forming the major portion of the court's jurisdiction, appeals are just not worth it to the majority of the parties involved. Also, the appeal mechanism is somewhat incestuous in some tribes, with one or more of the original trial judges sitting on the appeals court. At Wind River, however, an appeal is heard by a judge other than the one who heard the case originally.

Several problems plague the national tribal court system and its judges, especially the need for legal training for judges. Though community respect and personal integrity are admirable qualities, they are not sufficient for many of the issues which come before modern tribal judges. A number of groups have provided funds or training for tribal judges since the 1980s, including the Indian Law Support Center, the Native American Rights Fund, the Law Enforcement Assistance Administration, and the National American Indian Court Judges Association.[20]

Wind River tribal court judges are required to attend several hours per year of legal training, and as mentioned before, meet regularly to discuss cases and legal questions among themselves.

Other problems can sometimes include lack of adequate

---

19   The NAT Code includes a Peacemaking Court system for resolution of disputes that can include tribal elders.
20   John Schumacher, Shoshone Tribal Attorney, tape recorded interview with the author, Wind River Reservation, Wyoming, July, 1991.

administrative staff, enforcement of court orders, and undue influence and pressure and influence from interest groups such as the tribal council, religious leaders, and the BIA.[21] The "small town" atmosphere on many reservations, coupled with the informality of the tribal court system, can make it difficult for tribal judges to resist the influence of the reservation community.

The relationship of tribal courts to state and federal courts is a complicated issue. Normally, states honor one another's decisions under a reciprocity clause called "Full Faith and Credit"[22] However, Indian tribes are considered to be separate political bodies, distinct from states; therefore, the Full Faith and Credit obligation is not directly binding on the states. Nevertheless, state courts have ruled that tribal courts should be recognized with the same force as state courts as a matter of courtesy, or comity. To be granted comity, tribal courts need only demonstrate that the trial was fair and impartial. The issue of recognition of tribal court decisions is still evolving, but recent opinions of some state courts have held that the Full Faith and Credit clause should be extended to any territory of the United States, whether state, tribe or otherwise.[23] Indeed, Wyoming passed a law providing full faith and credit to certain judgements of the Wind River Tribal Court (excluding rulings under the Tribal Water Code).[24]

Disagreements over jurisdiction between the tribal court and other governmental entities, including the BIA, enforcement of court proceedings, and adequate funding and staffing of judicial offices are all difficulties of the Wind River judicial system. The 1987 Law and Order Code of tribes provides for a juvenile officer and a probation officer within the legal system. The Tribal Court is funded one-third by BIA monies and two-thirds by

---

21   Deloria, 123.
22   Deloria, 119.
23   Deloria, 120.
24   WY Stat § 5-1-111 (2024), Full Faith and Credit for Tribal Acts and Records.

tribal council monies. Court fines revert to the general fund of the Inter-Tribal Business Council and help offset the costs of the court system.

As in many other aspects of reservation life, the tribal courts are a curious and evolving mix of Indian and Anglo-American customs and procedures; the real question may be at which point the balance between the two is most beneficial to the tribes and to the American culture at large.

SUMMARY

There are many ways in which Indian government resembles the larger American government, and there are ways in which they are distinct. Government from tribe to tribe also varies significantly and generalizations about all tribal government based on the Wind River tribes should not be made.

The government of the Shoshones and Arapahos at Wind River resembles the representative democracy of the federal government, but the division of powers is not always as clear or as definite. The councils, and especially their chairmen, function broadly as the executive arm of the tribes, but even that function is different for each Tribe. The courts, of course, perform the primary judicial functions of the tribes, though they are not always the only arm of tribal government involved in judicial matters. Legislation has been sometimes a function of the tribal business councils, and sometimes not, since the 1930s.

Each tribe brings its own special slant to political activity on the reservation, with significant differences in philosophies of management, budgeting, and representation. The Arapahos, for example, empower their tribal council to enact legislation on their behalf. The Shoshone Tribe, however, retains legislative authority within its General Council. This duality of administration at Wind River, coupled with the BIA administrative role, poses singular challenges for the political representatives of

The Wind River Reservation Today, Wyoming Geographic
Information Science Center, University of Wyoming.

each Tribe, and particularly for the members of the Inter-Tribal
Business Council. Certainly, the governmental process is delayed
and complicated at times by the need to meet the needs of two
distinct political bodies of equal status and voting power, who
nevertheless must come to agreement about matters which affect
them both. Administration of land resources on the reservation is
just one example of necessary and important cooperative efforts.

Also, roles of the council and other governmental entities
change over time. Shoshone councilmen were allowed to pass
legislation on behalf of the Tribe prior to 1988, when the General
Council reclaimed its authority in that sphere. The power of the
BIA in tribal government also continues to ebb and flow over
time, though perhaps less so on the Wind River than other reservations which reorganized under 1934 IRA terms.

Finally, the political viewpoints of individual tribal members vary as they do in any large political group, and these
viewpoints sometimes crystallize into opposing factions within
the tribe. Issues as inclusive and far-reaching as Indian separat-
ism and sovereignty vs. assimilation and dependency are seen

in different ways by individual tribal members. Age, education, tribal affiliation, sex, and religious beliefs are only a few of the variables affecting Indian philosophies of government. The only thing which is virtually unanimous upon the reservation is a quiet pride in being Indian, and a desire to preserve Native American identity in the face of powerful forces from the outside which threaten to erode the heart of native culture. Just what that means for each individual in the twenty-first century, however, is a matter of individual interpretation.

The same political issues that plague Indians everywhere concern the Wind River tribes. Taxation, government-to-government relationships, land use, economic development, reapportionment and political representation, jurisdiction, and sovereignty of tribal governments are some of the main ones. Many national Indian groups, such as the Native American Rights Fund (NARF), are active Indian political coalitions on the national level. Indian state legislators are only now beginning to dialogue and organize to have an impact on Indian issues within state government.

The variable national economy, the decline of bureaucracy in organizations and its impact on reorganization of BIA, the information and technology revolution, changes in Indian demographics, the heightened demand for the country's natural resources, new political attitudes that favor the preservation of Indian culture and heritage, and an increasing global awareness are all factors that will come into play in the unfolding of Indian politics at all levels.

It is hard to say what tribal government will look like in 50 years on the reservation. Unquestionably, it will continue to reflect the government of the larger culture to the extent that its people interact with, are trained in, and accept those systems. The days are gone when total and complete isolation and autonomy are possible among the tribes. Ideally, the growth process of

Native American government, not only on the Wind River, but across the nation, might someday reflect a balance between the values of its varied cultures and the larger American culture that is beneficial and productive for all.

For Further Reading:

OVERVIEWS & REFERENCE (GENERAL FRAMEWORKS)
Canby, William C., Jr. *American Indian Law in a Nutshell.* 8th ed. West Academic Publishing, 2025. Compact, up-to-date coverage of federal Indian law that orients you to every major doctrine and policy area.

Pevar, Stephen L. *The Rights of Indians and Tribes.* 5th ed. Oxford University Press, 2024. Plain-language guide that explains tribal sovereignty, jurisdiction, and federal responsibilities, with recent case updates.

Cohen, Felix S. *Cohen's Handbook of Federal Indian Law.* 2012 ed., edited by Nell Jessup Newton et al. LexisNexis, 2012. The definitive legal treatise synthesizing statutes, treaties, and case law—indispensable for historical and doctrinal research.

Fletcher, Matthew L. M. *Federal Indian Law.* West Academic Publishing, 2016. Casebook-style analysis that traces the evolution of federal power and tribal sovereignty through leading decisions.

Conference of Western Attorneys General. *American Indian Law Deskbook.* 2024 ed. LegalWorks, 2024. Practical reference to jurisdiction, civil and criminal authority, and intergovernmental issues across Western states.

Deloria, Vine, Jr., and Clifford M. Lytle. *American Indians, American Justice.* University of Texas Press, 1983. Classic overview of how U.S. legal structures shape tribal governments and justice systems.

Richland, Justin B., and Sarah Deer. *Introduction to Tribal Legal Studies.* 2nd ed. AltaMira Press, 2010. Accessible primer on tribal courts, constitutions, and sovereignty for students and practitioners new to the field.

SOVEREIGNTY & FEDERAL–TRIBAL RELATIONS (SUPREME COURT DOCTRINES, FEDERAL POWER)

Wilkinson, Charles F. *American Indians, Time, and the Law: Native Societies in a Modern Constitutional Democracy.* Yale University Press, 1987. Explains how waves of Supreme Court doctrine have alternately constrained and recognized tribal self-government.

Wilkins, David E. *American Indian Sovereignty and the U.S. Supreme Court: The Masking of Justice.* University of Texas Press, 1997. Critical analysis of landmark cases that redefined the limits and meanings of tribal sovereignty.

Wilkins, David E., and K. Tsianina Lomawaima. *Uneven Ground: American Indian Sovereignty and Federal Law.* University of Oklahoma Press, 2001. Synthetic account showing how statutes and court decisions produce a patchwork of authority for Native nations.

Echo-Hawk, Walter R. *In the Courts of the Conqueror: The 10 Worst Indian Law Cases Ever Decided.* Oxford University Press, 2010. Historical critique of pivotal cases that curtailed tribal rights and altered reservation governance.

Wilkinson, Charles F. *Blood Struggle: The Rise of Modern Indian Nations.* W. W. Norton, 2005. Narrative history of the modern self-determination era that situates today's governance structures in federal policy shifts.

STATE–TRIBAL RELATIONS & PUBLIC LAW 280

Champagne, Duane, and Carole E. Goldberg. *Captured Justice: Native Nations and Public Law 280.* Carolina Academic Press, 2012. Empirical study of PL-280's transfer of jurisdiction to states and its consequences for public safety and governance.

Goldberg, Carole E., editor. *Planting Tail Feathers: Tribal Survival and Public Law 280*. UCLA American Indian Studies Center, 1997. Foundational essays detailing how tribes have navigated and resisted PL-280's jurisdictional impacts.

TRIBAL GOVERNANCE & NATION-BUILDING (CONSTITUTIONS, ADMINISTRATION, DEVELOPMENT)

Cohen, Felix S., edited by David E. Wilkins. *On the Drafting of Tribal Constitutions*. University of Oklahoma Press, 2006. Historical and practical guidance on structuring tribal governments and drafting constitutions that fit local priorities.

Fletcher, Matthew L. M. *American Indian Tribal Law*. 3rd ed. Aspen Publishing, 2024. Comprehensive treatment of internal tribal law—courts, legislative powers, and civil/criminal jurisdiction.

Jorgensen, Miriam, editor. *Rebuilding Native Nations: Strategies for Governance and Development*. University of Arizona Press, 2007. Nation-building manual emphasizing capable institutions, cultural match, and long-term development.

Richland, Justin B. *Cooperation without Submission: Indigenous Jurisdictions in Native Nation–US Engagements*. University of Chicago Press, 2021. Ethnographic-legal study of how tribes assert jurisdiction while coordinating with federal and state actors.

Pommersheim, Frank. *Braid of Feathers: American Indian Law and Contemporary Tribal Life*. University of California Press, 1995. Insightful essays exploring sovereignty in practice and the evolution of contemporary tribal governance.

TRIBAL COURTS & JUSTICE SYSTEMS

Pommersheim, Frank. *Tribal Justice: Twenty-Five Years as a Tribal Appellate Justice*. Carolina Academic Press, 2016. First-hand reflections from the tribal appellate bench illuminating doctrine, procedure, and judicial philosophy in Indian Country.

Richland, Justin B. *Cooperation without Submission: Indigenous Jurisdictions in Native Nation–US Engagements.* University of Chicago Press, 2021. Demonstrates how tribal courts and institutions manage interjurisdictional problems without ceding sovereign authority.

Deloria, Vine, Jr., and Clifford M. Lytle. *American Indians, American Justice.* University of Texas Press, 1983. Introduces the structure and purpose of tribal justice systems within the broader federal framework.

TRUST RESPONSIBILITY & ACCOUNTING (COBELL CONTEXT AND COVERAGE)

Pevar, Stephen L. *The Rights of Indians and Tribes.* 5th ed. Oxford University Press, 2024. Explains the federal trust responsibility and summarizes the litigation arc and outcomes of Cobell.

Canby, William C., Jr. *American Indian Law in a Nutshell.* 8th ed. West Academic Publishing, 2025. Concise explanation of trust doctrines, allotment legacies, and the policy backdrop to Cobell and related reforms.

Cohen, Felix S. *Cohen's Handbook of Federal Indian Law.* 2012 ed., edited by Nell Jessup Newton et al. LexisNexis, 2012. Authoritative sections on trust law, accounting, and fiduciary duties that frame the Cobell litigation.

INDIAN LAW IN WYOMING

Clayton, John. "Who Gets to Hunt Wyoming's Elk? Tribal Hunting Rights, U.S. Law and the 'Bannock War' of 1895." WyoHistory. org, 2020, accessed Aug. 22, 2025 at https://www.wyohistory.org/ encyclopedia/who-gets-hunt-wyomings-elk-tribal-hunting-rights-us-law-and-bannock-war-1895. In July 1895, a posse of non-Indians, mostly outfitters, attacked a peaceful band of Bannocks south of Jackson Hole. The Indians believed they were legally hunting elk off their Idaho reservation, but the U.S. Supreme Court ruled that state law overrode their treaty rights. In 2019, the court upended that decision in *Herrera v. Wyoming*, which involved a Crow Tribe member, also hunting in Wyoming and off his reservation.

MacKinnon, Anne. "Native Rights to Wind River Water." WyoHistory. org, 2019, accessed Aug. 22, 2025 at https://www.wyohistory.org/ encyclopedia/native-rights-wind-river-water. By treaty, Native Americans in 1868 were reserved land along—and water from— Wyoming's Wind River. But it would take a century and a half for courts to work out what water was whose—and to begin to define what tribal owners of the water could and couldn't use their water for.

Nickerson, Gregory. "Managing Game on the Wind River Reservation," WyoHistory.org, 2019, accessed Aug. 22, 2025 at https://www. wyohistory.org/encyclopedia/managing-game-wind-river-reservation. Tribal sovereignty and wildlife conservation on the Wind River Reservation, and circumstances surrounding the adoption of a tribal game code in 1984.

Chapter 6

INDIAN GAMING

Indian gaming is one of the most successful and heavily regulated activities in America today. An understanding of how this regulation developed is important in understanding its status in Wyoming. The history of gaming in Wyoming illustrates a decade-long and difficult struggle to exercise tribal sovereign authority. It also shows how tribal policy eventually can influence state law outside the reservation. For example, the idea of government-run gaming so resisted by the State, when it would be conducted by the Tribes, is now fully embraced in the Wyoming Lottery system.

INDIAN GAMING REGULATORY ACT (IGRA)

The foundation of federal law regarding gaming in Indian country is the Indian Gaming Regulatory Act of 1988 ("IGRA").[1] One of IGRA's primary purposes is to provide a "basis for the operation of gaming by Indian tribes as a means of promoting tribal economic development, self-sufficiency, and strong tribal governments." Its enactment followed a Supreme Court ruling in *California v. Cabazon Band of Mission Indians* upholding the right of tribes to operate and regulate gaming on their reservations if the kind of gaming is not expressly prohibited for all purposes by state law.[2]

---

1   25 U.S.C. 2701 *et seq*. Specific references to (or quotations from) IGRA are not otherwise cited in this chapter.

2   Most states (including Wyoming) lack authority to impose their criminal laws on Indians in Indian country. California is one of several states with criminal jurisdiction on Indian lands under a special federal statute known as "PL-280," which is why state criminal law applied to the Tribe in the *Cabazon* case.

In other words, if the gaming is a crime in that State, the Tribes there could not offer that gaming on their lands, but if the gaming is allowed, and merely regulated by the State, then the Tribes there could offer that same kind of gaming without all the restrictions of state regulation. The *Cabazon* decision is often cited as occasioning the enactment of IGRA and providing a backdrop for Indian gaming.

Although the revenue generated by specific tribal casinos varies depending on management, competition, and other factors, tribal gaming revenues nationwide have increased dramatically since the enactment of IGRA.[3]

IGRA recognizes the sovereign authority of tribes regarding gaming, but it also imposes the restriction mentioned above—tribes may not offer games which are completely prohibited by the state in which they are geographically located. IGRA also imposes a series of prerequisites to tribal gaming and empowers states, through the negotiation process, to gain concessions from tribes including, in many instances, substantial payments and state regulation of Indian gaming.

IGRA sets out three classes of gaming. Class I gaming means "social gaming solely for prizes of minimal value or traditional forms of Indian gaming ... in connection with tribal ceremonies or celebrations." This classification includes games of chance and skill that are played for minimal prizes, primarily fostering community and cultural engagement rather than generating significant revenue. Class I games are within the exclusive jurisdiction of the tribe and exempt from the provisions of IGRA.

Class II gaming includes (I) bingo and the following games if played at the same location as bingo: pull tabs, lotto, punch boards, tip jars, instant bingo and other games similar to bingo

---

3   In 1988, tribal gaming revenue was reported to be $212 million. By 1999, revenue had increased to $6.7 billion. (National Gambling Impact Study Commission Report, 1999), 2-9.

and (2) card games that "are not explicitly prohibited by the laws of the State" and conform to state regulation. Class II gaming does not include "any banking card games [games where the casino is one of the players], including baccarat, chemin de fer, or black-jack (21) or electronic or electromechanical facsimiles of any game of chance or slot machines of any kind." A tribe may offer Class II games for play if the state in which the tribe is located "permits such gaming for any purpose by any person," and no compact between the tribe and state is required for such games.

Class III gaming "means all forms of gaming that are not class I gaming or class II gaming." A tribe may offer Class III games if the state "permits such gaming for any purpose by any person," but a tribal-state compact, or the alternative processes set forth in IGRA, is required. Casino table games (roulette, craps, etc.) and slot machines are typical Class III games.

IGRA requires that all tribal gaming revenues be spent to fund tribal government, promote economic development, provide for the general welfare of the tribe and its members, or help fund charitable organizations and local governments.

Congress adopted IGRA to reconcile competing state and tribal interests. Tribes must seek a gaming compact (agreement), but the State must be able to show that it "negotiated with the Indian tribe in good faith to conclude a Tribal-State compact governing the conduct of gaming activities." This is an important part of the delicate balance Congress established under IGRA. Another part of that balance is the light-handed remedy for a state's failure to negotiate in good faith—the Court merely sends the state and the tribe back to the bargaining table, or to a mediator, or sends the tribe to the U.S. Secretary of the Interior for approval of class III gaming.

IGRA sets out a series of hurdles tribes must overcome in order to offer Class III gaming:

- Negotiations for a gaming compact must be initiated.

- If no compact is reached within 180 days, the tribe may consider filing suit for a judgment that the state failed to negotiate in good faith. If the state waives its immunity, the suit proceeds. (If the state asserts its sovereign immunity, the suit is dismissed, and the tribe must pursue alternative or "regulatory" gaming procedures established by the Secretary of Interior. These regulations are not referenced in IGRA.)[4]

- If a United States District Court rules that the state did not negotiate in good faith, the Court must order the tribe and state back to the bargaining table for another 60 days.

- If a compact still is not reached after the additional 60 days, the tribe may request appointment of a mediator under IGRA.

- The mediator attempts to resolve the issues between the parties in a further effort to reach a compact.

- If the mediator cannot get the parties to reach agreement, he must select either the tribe's or the state's last best offer for a compact; he cannot draft his own compact or mix and match terms from one proposal with another.

- Once a last best offer is selected, the state has another 60 days to accept or reject it. If the state accepts it, the parties move forward with a gaming compact. If the state rejects it, the mediator forwards it to the Secretary of the Department of the Interior for further action.

- The Secretary must "prescribe" federal Class III gaming procedures for the tribe which are consistent with the last best offer selected by the mediator.

If no compact is reached because a state fails to negotiate in

---

4   As discussed later, one court (in Texas) has said the Secretary was not authorized to establish these "regulatory" gaming procedures.

good faith, the state loses considerable leverage over the tribe. Secretarial procedures will not necessarily include any concessions to state interests (other than the broad restriction under IGRA that the tribe may not offer games which the State prohibits all others from offering under any circumstances). In addition, IGRA permits states to file a lawsuit against tribes only if the state alleges violation of a compact; enforcement of a tribe's Secretarial gaming procedures is purely a federal matter.

INITIAL NEGOTIATIONS AT WIND RIVER
(JANUARY, 1995 – APRIL, 2000)

The Northern Arapaho Tribe (NAT) first requested formal gaming negotiations with Wyoming pursuant to IGRA in 1995. That same year, the Tribe enacted the Northern Arapaho Gaming Code,[5] which was approved by the National Indian Gaming Commission. The Tribe also established the Northern Arapaho Gaming Agency ("NAGA"). Despite these efforts, legal issues created by IGRA and opposition from a Wyoming Senator and Governor blocked the Tribe's efforts to develop gaming during this period.

Wyoming Governor Jim Geringer rejected any gaming by the Tribe that was not in strict conformity with state law and, in fact, sought additional restrictions not applicable to anyone under state law. The Governor insisted (at first) that he needed authorization from the Wyoming legislature to enter into a gaming compact.[6] The Tribe began to lay the groundwork for state legislation as well as a lawsuit in late 1995.

In 1996, the United States Supreme Court ruled that States

---

5   NAT Code, Title 3, S:\C NABC 94-65\Laws-NAT 04\Northern Arapaho Code 04.02\Code (final) 04.02.02\No Arap Code WP\NA Code Title 3 Gaming 3-31-17. wp.

6   *Wind River News*, Vol. 20 No. 6, February 6, 1997. The Governor's approach was criticized by several legislators; the late Senator Vinich said "The governor Pinocchio speaks with a forked tongue..."

could assert sovereign immunity from lawsuits filed under IGRA.[7] Tribes were stranded by the ruling—they now had critical rights without a remedy against any state that was determined to prevent Indian gaming. Until "alternative" procedures were developed by regulation in 1999, the Supreme Court decision, coupled with Governor Geringer's refusal to negotiate consistent with IGRA, effectively prevented the NAT from offering any class III gaming.

The Tribe pressed forward with efforts to negotiate a solution. Although the Tribe did not necessarily agree that legislation was required for Governor Geringer to enter into a gaming compact, the Tribe engaged in educational and lobbying efforts in the State Legislature which culminated in a bill that passed the State Senate in 1997. Despite significant support in the legislature, the Governor succeeded in defeating the bill in the closing days of the legislative session. Despite his earlier position, the Governor *then* argued to the House and Senate that legislation was *not* necessary. The bill would have confirmed his authority to enter into a compact and opened the way for a wide variety of class III gaming by the NAT.[8]

For three years, Senator Michael Enzi (R-Wyo.) led a successful effort to impose a moratorium on the implementation of any "alternative" procedures for class III gaming by the Secretary.[9] Without alternative procedures in instances when a state asserts sovereign immunity, the Tribe was again denied a way to obtain class III gaming under IGRA. The NAT was effectively blocked by the combined efforts of Governor Geringer and Senator Enzi

---

7   *Seminole Tribe of Florida v. Florida*, 517 U.S. 44 (1996).

8   *Wind River News*, Vol.20 No. 6, February 6, 1997. "Prompted in part by a strongly worded letter from the governor, the Senate on Wednesday killed a pair of bills designed to pave the way for casino-type gaming on the Wind River Indian Reservation."

9   Department of Interior appropriation bills in fiscal years 1998, 1999, and 2000.

until 2000.

The Tribe spent this time improving its gaming infrastructure, including its regulations and training for members of NAGA. It also successfully litigated for its right to use electronic Class II pull tab games at its casino, which did not require a compact and provided significant new revenue for the Tribe.[10]

RENEWED NEGOTIATIONS
(MAY, 2000 – NOVEMBER, 2000)

Senator Enzi did not succeed in imposing a moratorium on "alternative" procedures in fiscal year 2001 (which began in October of 2000). In anticipation of this development, the Tribe hired a consultant with extensive experience in the gaming industry to assist in developing a more profitable class II gaming operation and to play a key role in renewed negotiations for class III gaming and press relations.[11]

The NAT again requested gaming negotiations with the State pursuant to the IGRA in 2000. The Tribe sought negotiations on a list of games expressly permitted by state statute, including "contests of skill," raffles, pull tabs, "any game, wager or transaction" for "social purposes," "calcutta," and "parimutuel wagering."[12] Wyoming refused to negotiate for any gaming under the state law categories of "contests of skill" or "any game, wager or transaction." The State would only negotiate for raffles, pull tabs, calcutta and parimutuel wagering under the strict conditions applicable to those games as a matter of state law and also insisted on restrictions not applicable to the games under state law. The imposition of these conditions were contrary to the express language of IGRA.

Governor Geringer again took the position that legislation

---

10   *Seneca-Cayuga, Fort Sill Apache, Northern Arapaho Tribe and Diamond Games v. NIGC*, 327 F.3d 1019 (10th Cir. 2003).

11   Howell Strategic Consulting.

12   W.S. § 6-7-101(a) and §§ 11-25-101 *et seq.*

was needed to authorize him to enter into a compact. (Such legislation was not required for Tribal-State agreements regarding fuel taxes, social services, and other matters.) Nonetheless, when the Governor announced his intent to seek legislation to address gaming issues, the Tribe welcomed that position because it meant the parties no longer needed to litigate which games would be included in a compact—rather, the parties could focus on economic, social, regulatory and other governmental concerns. The issues would be moved to a larger legislative arena. The Tribe again became more active in communications with the legislature and invited State Senate and House leadership to negotiations in anticipation of legislative action.

While the Governor insisted that legislation was needed, he would not take advantage of the opportunity that legislation offered to resolve the issues. After the Governor insisted on legislative involvement, the Attorney General advised several legislators in writing *not to attend any negotiation sessions.* The Attorney General even opined that attendance would subject the legislator to *personal liability* to the Tribe if a compact was not achieved.[13] (Nothing in IGRA would create such liability.) The Governor rejected the Tribe's proposed legislation authorizing him to compact, insisting instead that the compact first had to be negotiated in strict conformity with his view of state law and then approved by the legislature in the exact form in which it had been negotiated.

NAT'S FEDERAL COMPLAINT UNDER IGRA
(NOVEMBER, 2000 – FEBRUARY, 2002)

More than 180 days elapsed without a gaming compact. The Tribe then filed suit under IGRA in November 2000, seeking a

---

13   March 15, 2002, letter from Chief Deputy Attorney General Celeste Colgan to Representative Harry Tipton and other legislators. ("...any legislator on the [negotiating] team would likely be sued in his individual capacity.").

declaration that the State had failed to negotiate in good faith and for an order returning the parties to the bargaining table under the process set forth under IGRA.

The State filed an Answer and its own request for a ruling in its favor and waived its immunity from suit in December, 2000. (By that time, the moratorium on alternative procedures Senator Enzi put in place had expired.)

By March, 2001, all issues had been briefed and argued to the U.S. District Court. During the next eleven months, the Tribe worked diligently to ensure its compliance with federal and tribal gaming regulations. Management at 789 Casino changed and the Tribe hired a new CEO, who turned a marginally profitable business into a multi-million-dollar enterprise.[14] The Tribe authorized its "Gaming Task Force," which led a series of developments to further refine and improve accountability and profitability of the Tribe's gaming facilities. The District Court issued its judgment on February 6, 2002.

The State had argued that the Tribe was not a "Tribe" for purposes of IGRA because the Northern Arapaho share owner-ship of the Wind River Reservation with the Eastern Shoshone Tribe (EST). The State argued that it need only negotiate with *both* tribes and, because the Shoshone had not pursued gaming, the State was not obligated to enter into *any* gaming negotiations. The District Court ruled against the State, saying that the State must negotiate under IGRA with the Northern Arapaho.[15]

The District Court found that Wyoming failed to negoti-ate in good faith because it refused to negotiate for calcutta and parimutuel wagering other than in conformity with state law restrictions or regulations which do not apply to tribes under

---

14   David T. Staddon, retired Vice President of Marketing at Soaring Eagle, the second largest Indian casino in the country, managed 789 Casino for over a year to jump start NAT's management profile.

15   *Northern Arapaho Tribe v. Geringer*, 2002 WL 31961497 at *3.

IGRA. The District Court made it clear that regarding the kinds of games allowed, the Tribe is entitled to much more, not less, than what state law permits. "The subject of negotiations would be whether the tribe could offer such gaming in an Indian-run casino, not whether the tribe could offer such gaming in conformance with the state statute. If the latter were the case, there would not be reason to negotiate because the tribe could clearly operate gaming under the restrictions of the existing state statute without negotiating with the state."[16] Negotiations "must not be limited to the scope that Wyoming allows under the law."[17] "Wyoming has a duty to negotiate for terms beyond that which Wyoming law expressly permits."[18]

The Court also found that the State was not required to negotiate regarding tribally-operated "casino-style" games or "[slot] machines." The Court ordered the parties to return to the bargaining table for another 60 days pursuant to the procedures set forth in IGRA.

The State filed a request that the Court amend its judgment, which the Court denied in March, 2002. The State then filed a Motion to Stay Proceedings Pending Appeal and the Court set the matter for hearing in April, 2002. By then, the additional 60 day period for compact negotiations had expired.

On April 19, 2002, the Court issued a written order denying the State's Motion to Stay Proceedings Pending Appeal and issued its Order Appointing retired federal judge James Carrigan as Mediator pursuant to IGRA.

Wyoming appealed and the Tribe filed a protective cross-appeal to the District Court order (the Tribe appealed that part of the ruling that said it could not operate slot machines). The Tenth Circuit Mediation Office stayed the briefing schedule

---

16   Ibid. at fn.5.
17   Ibid. at *10.
18   Ibid.

at least until the court-appointed Mediator either brokered an agreement or chose a compact proposal.

THE IGRA MEDIATION
(APRIL, 2002 – DECEMBER, 2002)

If a federal court rules that a state has failed to negotiate in good faith, IGRA requires that states and tribes then enter into a mediation phase. At the direction of the federal Mediator, the State and Tribe submitted extensive briefing and supporting documents and provided oral argument and discussion on virtually every aspect and issue of the competing gaming proposals.

One area of disagreement thoroughly argued before the Mediator was whether any "casino-style" gaming could be conducted on the Reservation. The District Court order prohibited the *Tribe* from offering it directly, but also ruled that the State allows *others* to offer "such [casino] gaming for any purpose; namely, a social one." The Tribe argued that (at a minimum) non-profit organizations should be permitted to offer casino-style gaming on the Reservation at the Tribe's facility just as they do elsewhere in the State.

The NAT had commissioned a six-year study which documented extensive evidence of "casino nights" operated by non-profit organizations across Wyoming.[19] The study focused on games like roulette, poker, dice, blackjack, and poker. The study included direct observations and participation by the investigator in casino gaming in several counties in 1995-1996, including those at which local and even law enforcement officials participated, and found 111 gambling events over 14 months and 214 separate advertisements or news stories about these events. During the same period, the study found no law enforcement action against *any* of the 111 public gambling events. Twenty-six samples of advertisements or news stories were included in the

---

19   Investigation conducted by Steve Wiles of Rancher's Realty.

report, many showing headlines and photographs of players at the casino games. Samples of recent photographs and coverage of the "casino nights" also were submitted to the Mediator.

The Tribe saw no reason similar organizations could not conduct these same "casino nights" at the Tribe's facility, and the Mediator agreed.

Another area of disagreement argued before the Mediator was what technology the Tribe could use in connection with the games it would offer. Off-track betting in Wyoming used machines with bill-acceptors, video displays, touch-screen technology, and computers for placing bets, communicating with off-site computers, calculating wins and losses, holding credits for patrons, and creating and printing bar codes on vouchers. Nonetheless, the State's proposal prohibited all such technology for tribal gaming. Even simple machines used at carnivals in Wyoming would not be allowed. The Tribe argued that technological aids and facsimiles were lawful under IGRA so long as the game being played was permitted under State law.

In November, 2002, the Mediator acknowledged that he was "required to select from the two proposals submitted by the State of Wyoming and the Northern Arapaho Tribe the one which best comports with the terms of the Act [IGRA], any other applicable federal law, and the findings and order of the District Court." The Mediator chose the Last Best Offer of the Tribe pursuant to the requirements of IGRA.

In December, 2002, as one of his last official acts, Governor Geringer rejected the NAT's Last Best Offer and asked the Mediator "...under the provisions of [IGRA]... to notify the Secretary of the Interior of the non-consent of the State of Wyoming to the Tribe's proposed compact." The Tribe joined in this request and the Mediator sent the Tribe's Last Best Offer to the Department of the Interior in December, 2002.

SECRETARIAL GAMING "PROCEDURES" (JANUARY, 2003 – NOVEMBER, 2004; 2007; AND 2014 AMENDMENTS)

Federal regulations detail what a proposal requesting Class III gaming procedures should contain when a Tribe has filed a lawsuit against a State under IGRA, the State has asserted sovereign immunity, and the suit has been dismissed—the "alternative" procedures process. These regulations were not applicable to the Northern Arapaho proposal because Wyoming had waived its immunity from suit, was found to have negotiated in bad faith, and the IGRA Mediator requested Class III procedures directly under the terms of IGRA.[20] Nonetheless, the Tribe submitted its proposal and relevant information in a format similar to that required by the regulations.

The Tribe's proposal for federal Class III gaming procedures, although based on the Last Best Offer of the Tribe approved by the Court-appointed IGRA Mediator, notably did not contain any provisions for State involvement.

At this point in the IGRA process, the Secretary "shall prescribe" procedures in consultation with the Tribe *only*—the State has no role at this final stage. The proposal reflected the fact that it had been rejected by the State and that no gaming compact was or would be in effect.

In January, 2003, Senator Enzi tried again to frustrate the rights of the Tribe; he sought to introduce an appropriations rider similar to those he successfully sponsored in 1998- 2000. As a result of efforts by the Tribe and its lobbyist, Senator Enzi faced significant resistance and withdrew his effort.[21]

---

20   The "alternative" or "regulatory" procedures only applied when a state asserted sovereign immunity and the federal lawsuit had been dismissed.

21   "Enzi, who opposes gambling, is looking at blocking the [Indian] casino with an amendment to a spending bill in Congress." *AP Casper, Wyoming,* January 15, 2003. Enzi "has decided not to offer an amendment that would have prohibited...class III gaming [procedures] for the Northern Arapaho Tribe." *Wyoming Eagle-Tribune,* January 23, 2003 (Nation, p. A4).

Tribal representatives met with officials from the Department of Interior, Office of the Solicitor, and the National Indian Gaming Commission. Several federal representatives resisted the issuance of procedures without State regulation of gaming by the Tribe—this had been done only once before in the history of IGRA (*Mashantucket Pequot v. Connecticut* case) and those procedures were quickly outdated when that state and tribe reached a gaming compact. The Northern Arapaho Tribe presented a case that did not match any other model.

After repeated efforts to overcome this resistance, federal officials agreed in November of 2004, that Wyoming could have no role in the oversight of gaming by the Tribe. A memorandum of understanding ("MOU") was reached between the Tribe, Interior, and the NIGC to provide for NIGC oversight instead of State involvement. *No other Tribe had achieved Class III gaming without significant concessions to their states, including state regulation and significant payments of gaming revenue by the tribe to the state.*

NAT expanded its casino operations and broke ground for construction of the Wind River Casino in 2004. [22] In 2007, NAT Class III gaming procedures underwent amendments to expand gaming and floor sizes. In 2014, the expiration date of the procedures was extended through December 31, 2040. [23]

TENTH CIRCUIT COURT RULING (2004)

The NAT and the State had agreed that the appeal process could wait at least until after the IGRA mediation had been completed. After the mediation, the Tribe and Wyoming presented their arguments to the Court of Appeals. In November of 2004, the

---

22   Wind River Casino's opening ceremony was April 4, 2009.
23   The Tribe's gaming procedures can be found at Arapaho Tribe of the Wind River Reservation Gaming Procedures | Indian Affairs (bia.gov). Because they are the only *procedures*, they are listed among the compacts entered into by other tribes.

Court ruled that *the Tribe is entitled to the "full gamut of any game, wager or transaction"* and that the State did indeed negotiate with the Tribe in bad faith.[24] That finally put to rest the gaming rights of the NAT.

SHOSHONE GAMING COMPACT (2006)

After years of struggle by the NAT and approval of the Tribe's Class III gaming procedures, Governor Freudenthal quickly reached a gaming compact with the Eastern Shoshone Tribe on terms similar to those in the NAT gaming procedures.[25] The compact provided some additional gaming floor space and flexibility, which the NAT later obtained through an amendment to its federal gaming procedures.

THE TRIBES' VIRTUAL MONOPOLY (2005–2019)

Because Wyoming prohibited gaming for profit,[26] the Tribes enjoyed a virtual monopoly on casino-style gaming for several years. The State ranked second-highest in tribal casino growth rates in the United States in 2009.[27] The NAT casinos employed about 700 people,[28] 80% of whom were members of the Tribe.[29] News stories described how tribal casinos and other state casinos were tapping into multi-million-dollar gaming expenditures by Wyoming residents.[30] In 2013, the legislature authorized the state-sponsored lottery, which began operations the following year.[31] Forces within the State urged the legislature to open gaming so others could compete with tribal gaming and so the State

24   *Northern Arapaho Tribe v. Geringer*, 429 F.3d 934 (10th Cir. 2005) (*en banc*).
25   The EST compact can be found at Eastern Shoshone Tribe of the Wind River Reservation Tribal State Gaming Compact | Indian Affairs (bia.gov).
26   Because tribes are governments, tribal gaming revenue is not "for profit."
27   *Billings Gazette*, April 11, 2011.
28   *Riverton Ranger*, October 17, 2014.
29   *Casper Star-Tribune*, May 27, 2019.
30   Wyoming residents spent $33million in Deadwood, South Dakota, alone in 2003. *Casper Star-Tribune*, December 16, 2004, at A1 and A6.
31   *Riverton Ranger*, February 2, 2014.

could tax off-reservation gaming revenue. During the 2017–2018 sessions, the NAT lobbied the Wyoming Legislature, successfully preventing the expansion of off-reservation gaming that would have competed directly with the Tribe's Class III casinos.

NAT CHANGES COURSE (2019–2024)

After an investigative article published in the *Casper Star-Tribune* in August 2019 asserted the Northern Arapaho Business Council (NABC) had created a secret lobbying firm to prevent further expansion of off-reservation gaming, the highly divided NABC leadership changed course, condemning lobbying efforts made on its behalf and publicly supporting the expansion of off-reservation gaming.[32] Reflecting the conflicts within the NABC leadership, the NAT took this new position despite projected losses to the Tribe of $14 million a year, nearly 40% of its revenue.[33]

In 2020, Wyoming amended its laws to allow "skill based" machines that simulate slot machines[34] and taxes that revenue. Several locations across the State now compete with the NAT and EST casinos using games that look like casino-style machines[35] and that, until this law legalized the use of what the Attorney General had previously considered to be slot machines.[36]

In 2022, NAT proposed that the State allow it to operate a casino in Cheyenne and split the revenue with the state to

---

32   *Casper Star-Tribune*, August 4, 2019, A1, A8-9.
33   Ibid.
34   W.S. §11-25-301.
35   In one corner of the gaming screen, the tail end of a historic horse race is played. Players "select three out of 10 horses that competed in a historic horse race. Or they opt out to have the computer" make the selection. "In the center [of the screen], a reel spun with iconic sevens and cherries reminiscent of Las Vegas-style slot machines…[and] many legislators described the terminals as slot machines." *Casper Star-Tribune*, August 16, 2014.
36   Wyoming Attorney General Formal Opinion 2018-0002. "Instant racing" had "a terminal that looked like a slot machine and was used like a slot machine" and was therefore illegal.

help solve a perpetual shortfall in education funding.[37] Despite making a case that the NAT had by far the most experience in casino development and management, no such deal materialized.

In June 2024, The Horse Palace at Swan Ranch, managed by Wyoming Horse Racing, opened just south of Cheyenne, a few miles from the Colorado border. Wyoming Horse Racing was acquired by Pacesetter Racing & Gaming, shortly before opening the 30,000-square-foot facility, estimating between 70% and 75% of their customers will come from the Colorado market. Pacesetter plans to open another Wyoming-based casino on the other end of the state, in Evanston near the Utah border. The Swan Ranch facility is estimated to produce between $2.6 million and $3 million in tax dollars to be split among the state, county, and city.[38] As of 2025, there are no agreements between the NAT or EST and the State of Wyoming to allow them to establish an off-reservation casino.

37   *Cowboy State Daily*, November 21, 2022.
38   *Wyoming Tribune Eagle*, "Horse Palace Swan Ranch Opens its Doors," https://www.wyomingnews.com/news/local_news/horse-palace-swan-ranch-opens-its-doors/article_d9b383ce-3036-11ef-99c0-cfd74640dc00.html; *Rocky Mountain Collegian*, September 10, 2024. https://collegian.com/sponsored/2024/09/will-the-new-wyoming-casino-attract-north-colorado-gamblers/

For Further Reading:

CORE LEGAL OVERVIEWS & TREATISES

Rand, Kathryn R. L., and Steven Andrew Light. *Indian Gaming Law and Policy*. 3rd ed. Durham, N.C.: Carolina Academic Press, 2025. The leading single-volume treatment of IGRA and tribal–state compacts, updated with recent cases and regulatory practice.

Rand, Kathryn R. L., and Steven Andrew Light. *Indian Gaming Law: Cases and Materials*. 2nd ed. Durham, N.C.: Carolina Academic Press, 2019. The standard casebook that traces the doctrine from pre-IGRA decisions through compacting, regulation, and enforcement.

Eadington, William R., editor. *Indian Gaming and the Law*. Reno: University of Nevada Press, 2002. An early comprehensive collection that links legal rules to economic and policy impacts in the IGRA era.

Miller, Keith C., editor. *The Law of Regulated Gambling: A Practical Guide for Business Lawyers*. Chicago: American Bar Association, 2020. Broad regulated-gaming reference with chapters on tribal gaming that clarify compliance, licensing, and operational issues.

Gaming Law & Practice. current ed. LexisNexis. A practitioner reference with coverage of tribal gaming frameworks alongside commercial and state regimes.

POLICY, POLITICS, AND HISTORY OF INDIAN GAMING

Light, Steven Andrew, and Kathryn R. L. Rand. *Indian Gaming and Tribal Sovereignty: The Casino Compromise*. Lawrence: University Press of Kansas, 2008. Explains how IGRA balanced sovereignty and regulation, shaping the modern tribal gaming landscape.

Mason, W. Dale. *Indian Gaming: Tribal Sovereignty and American Politics*. Norman: University of Oklahoma Press, 2000. Analyzes how gaming reconfigured federal, state, and tribal power relations and mobilized new political coalitions.

Hansen, Kenneth N., and Tracy A. Skopek. *The New Politics of Indian Gaming: The Rise of Reservation Interest Groups.* Reno: University of Nevada Press, 2011. Shows how tribal gaming catalyzed sophisticated interest-group strategies in local and state politics.

Benedict, Jeff. *Without Reservation: The Making of America's Most Powerful Indian Tribe and Foxwoods, the World's Largest Casino.* New York: HarperCollins, 2000. A narrative case study (Mashantucket Pequot/Foxwoods) illustrating the legal, financial, and political stakes of large-scale tribal gaming.

KEY STATUTORY BACKDROP (FOR REFERENCE)

United States Congress. *Indian Gaming Regulatory Act.* Pub. L. No. 100-497 1988. The foundational statute establishing the Class I–III framework, tribal–state compacts, and federal oversight through the NIGC.

Appendix To Chapter 6

INDIAN GAMING PRIMER

This one-page overview outlines the core legal framework for gaming on tribal lands under the Indian Gaming Regulatory Act (IGRA) and related practice.

LEGAL FOUNDATION

• *California v. Cabazon Band of Mission Indians* (1987) limited state authority over tribal bingo and catalyzed Congress to enact IGRA in 1988.

• IGRA's purposes: promote tribal economic development, self-sufficiency, and strong governments; ensure fair and honest gaming; and shield gaming from corrupt influences.

IGRA CLASSES & WHO REGULATES

• Class I (social/ceremonial): exclusively regulated by tribes.

• Class II (bingo and certain non-banked card games): allowed where the state permits such gaming; regulated by tribes with National Indian Gaming Commission (NIGC) oversight; no compact required.

• Class III (casino-style: slots, banked cards, roulette, etc.): requires a tribal–state compact approved by the U.S. Department of the Interior (DOI).

THE REGULATORY TRIAD

• Tribal: Tribal Gaming Regulatory Authority (TGRA) licenses employees, enforces tribal gaming ordinances, and ensures Minimum Internal Control Standards (MICS).

• Federal: NIGC approves tribal gaming ordinances, audits, and can impose civil fines or closure orders; DOI reviews and approves Class III compacts.

• State: Exercises only compact-based oversight (e.g., inspections, technical standards) agreed to by the tribe and approved by DOI.

COMPACTS, REVENUE, AND LAND STATUS
• Compacts set the rules for Class III (scope of games, audits, technical standards, allocation of regulatory roles, and—where lawful—revenue-sharing linked to meaningful concessions).

• Net gaming revenues may fund tribal government, community welfare, economic development, charitable donations, and local government services; per-capita distributions require an approved revenue allocation plan.

• Gaming on lands acquired after 1988 is generally barred unless an IGRA exception applies (e.g., restored lands, land-claim settlements, initial reservation) or DOI issues 'two-part determination' procedures with a governor's concurrence.

CURRENT ISSUES TO WATCH
• Sports betting and iGaming are typically Class III and require compact authority; mobile wagering often hinges on how 'on-reservation' play is defined in compacts/state law.

• Post-*Seminole* limits on suing states for bad-faith negotiations make Secretarial procedures a narrow, case-specific path for Class III in some jurisdictions.

• PL-280 and state criminal/prohibitory vs. civil/regulatory distinctions still drive jurisdictional outcomes in Indian Country.